FREEING ALI

THE HUMAN FACE OF THE PACIFIC SOLUTION

Michael Gordon is national editor of *The Age*. His books include
A True Believer: Paul Keating and *Reconciliation: A Journey*. He is a
research associate of the Swinburne Institute for Social Research.

BRIEFINGS

A series of topical books exploring social, political
and cultural issues in contemporary Australia

Series editors: Peter Browne and Julian Thomas
Australian Policy Online (www.apo.org.au)
Institute for Social Research, Swinburne University of Technology

Details of recent Briefings books appear at the back of this book

Freeing Ali

THE HUMAN FACE OF THE PACIFIC SOLUTION

MICHAEL GORDON

UNSW
PRESS

A UNSW Press book

Published by
University of New South Wales Press Ltd
University of New South Wales
Sydney NSW 2052
AUSTRALIA
www.unswpress.com.au

National Library of Australia
Cataloguing-in-Publication entry

Gordon, Michael, 1955– .

Freeing Ali: the human face of the Pacific solution.

ISBN 0 86840 978 2.

1. Mullaie, Ali. 2. Refugees – Government policy – Australia. 3. Asylum, Right of – Australia. 4. Australia – Relations – Nauru. 5. Nauru – Relations – Australia. I. Title. (Series: Briefings (University of New South Wales Press))

323.6310994

Cover photograph: Sandy Scheltema, courtesy of *The Age*

Contents

Foreword

Petro Georgiou MP

Since the colonisation of Australia, our attitudes towards newcomers have ranged across the spectrum from welcome to hostility, from generosity to rejection. Policies towards immigrants have been driven in part by optimism and idealism, and also by fear.

"Populate or perish" became the blunt shorthand term for the idea that Australia's very survival demanded a rapid increase in population. It was particularly potent after the second world war, to the extent that Australia began to actively search for migrants beyond the traditional sources.

Over the past 50 years, Australia has taken in five and a half million people from over 130 countries, and created a strikingly cohesive and diverse society. As I reflect on the extent of the successive waves of migration over the half century, and the changes in the composition of the intake during that period, I am in awe of the astonishing ability of our society to make it a success.

There have always been problems, pain, hardships, controversies and dislocation. There always will be. But most striking of all is the undeniable reality that our postwar experience with migration has been uniquely successful, and Australia is a stronger nation because of it.

The arrivals have not always been invited. Thirty years ago, in the early months of the Fraser government, five young Vietnamese men landed at Darwin on a small wooden boat after two months at sea. Over the next five years more than 50 other boats arrived, carrying over 2000 Vietnamese people. Public opinion was divided but generally sympathetic. The immigration department proposed the establishment of a "minimal detention facility" centre in northern Australia. This was firmly rejected by the government, which was committed to honouring our obligations to refugees from a conflict to which Australia had been a party. Despite formidable linguistic, educational and other challenges, overwhelmingly the settlement of Vietnamese people of refugee and other backgrounds has been a success story for them and for the Australian community at large.

Since 1992, Australian policies towards refugees and asylum seekers have been magnanimous to the invited and punitive to the uninvited. Refugees selected from overseas for resettlement in Australia have been treated with considerable generosity and compassion. Internationally, the assistance we provide them is second to none. In contrast, the arrival by boat of unauthorised asylum seekers saw the introduction of mandatory detention, temporary protection visas, and the so-called Pacific Solution, which is the focus of *Freeing Ali*. Asylum seekers were characterised as "queue-jumpers." Policy makers and the public feared that the number who saw Australia as a desirable destination was too big to accommodate and, since September 11, that terrorists might be hiding among them.

Thankfully, the atmosphere of crisis which saw the introduction of severe measures has passed. Two factors significantly eased the sense of alarm which sustained these policies. One is that the outcomes about which people were most worried did not eventuate – boats and asylum seekers stopped coming and, overwhelmingly, those who had made it turned out to be bona fide refugees.

The second factor that has eased the sense of alarm is that more and more Australians have got to know the "boat people" as real people like themselves, not a faceless threatening horde – as people willing to apply their strength and skills in a variety of occupations; as friends and neighbours and musicians and able members of sporting teams.

As we got to know them, we have been moved by the stories of why and how refugees fled their countries of origin and undertook harrowing journeys to reach Australia, of what they found here, both the positive and negative: for many, sometimes lengthy periods of detention in harsh settings, followed by the insecurity and anguish of temporary protection visas, and denial of the right to be reunited with family members.

By showing the human face of the "boat people" (to borrow from the subtitle of this book), journalists like Michael Gordon have played a vital role in easing public anxieties and creating the climate for the significant changes in policy which have recently been implemented.

Freeing Ali demonstrates why Michael Gordon has earned a reputation as one of Australia's most respected journalists. Over three decades of reporting here and overseas, Michael has exemplified a combination of professional objectivity complemented by empathy and humanity. In the finest traditions of his profession, he deploys his investigative, analytical and writing skills to expose injustice and prick the conscience of the community.

Five years ago, following a six week solo trip visiting indigenous communities, he wrote a series of newspaper articles which formed the foundation of his book *Reconciliation: A Journey*. *Freeing Ali* follows the same pattern. After repeated requests for permission, Michael was the first journalist to be given unfettered access to the Nauruan facility and wrote a very moving account published in *The Age*.

The main protagonists of *Freeing Ali* are the people who have been detained on Nauru for years. Michael's portraits of individuals evocatively depict their desperate search for peace and security for themselves and their families. If the uninvited offend against our preference for an orderly migration process, these stories persuasively elucidate why escaping from persecution is not an orderly process.

Freeing Ali describes the destructive effects of the years of uncertainty, frustration and fear people have spent and continue to spend languishing on Nauru. The book also tells the stories of Australians who have assisted the Nauruan detainees. Many of them are not public figures. They do what they do not professionally, but simply in response to their plight of fellow human beings. These are people who are sometimes described as "ordinary." Their hard work, generosity and empathy show them to be extraordinary.

The recently announced changes to the treatment of asylum seekers and refugees are a tribute to the persistent and tenacious advocacy of thousands of Australian citizens. Their letters, emails, phone calls and personal visits constantly remind parliamentarians that a significant section of the community to whom we are accountable cares passionately about the impact of our nation's policies on the individuals most immediately affected by them: asylum seekers and refugees.

Although the recent changes do not apply to Nauru, the shifts in Australian sentiment have had an impact. I am hopeful that Michael Gordon's account of the Nauruan detainees will hasten a compassionate and speedy response to the situation of the 30 or so who remain at the time of writing.

Aslam Kazimi, who was recently admitted to Australia after more than three years detained on Nauru, tells Michael Gordon that his journey began when he fled Afghanistan at age 13 and it "will not be complete until the time of my being reunited with my family." In its recent treatment of certain asylum seekers and refugees, Australia has also been on a journey, one which will not be completed until all those remaining are freed and given the opportunity to rebuild their lives.

Introduction

What we have is the Minister for Defence saying in the immediate post-Tampa environment, "Don't humanise the refugees."

– SENATE REPORT ON CHILDREN OVERBOARD AFFAIR, OCTOBER 2002

The day Ali Yawar Mullaie was to leave Nauru and begin a new life in Australia, he was asked to call by the office of the second most senior minister in the Nauruan government, David Adeang, and pick up a reference. For more than three years, Mullaie had simultaneously been a detainee at a refugee processing centre and a volunteer teacher in the Nauru education system. In 2005, his students included Adeang's son and the daughter of the education minister, Baron Waqa. He may have been rejected three times by Australian immigration officials before his claim for refugee status was finally accepted in mid-2005, but he made an indelible impression on the tiny, near bankrupt cauldron that is Nauru.

Adeang's reference was glowing. It began by saying that Ali Mullaie had been well known to the government and people of Nauru for almost four years. "He has endeared himself well with the community, particularly the teachers and students of Nauru with whom he was closely associated as a teacher – at the Aiwo Primary School, at the Arubo Catholic Mission and finally at Nauru College. He is of friendly and personable demeanour, and this allowed him to make many friends in Nauru, of all ages.

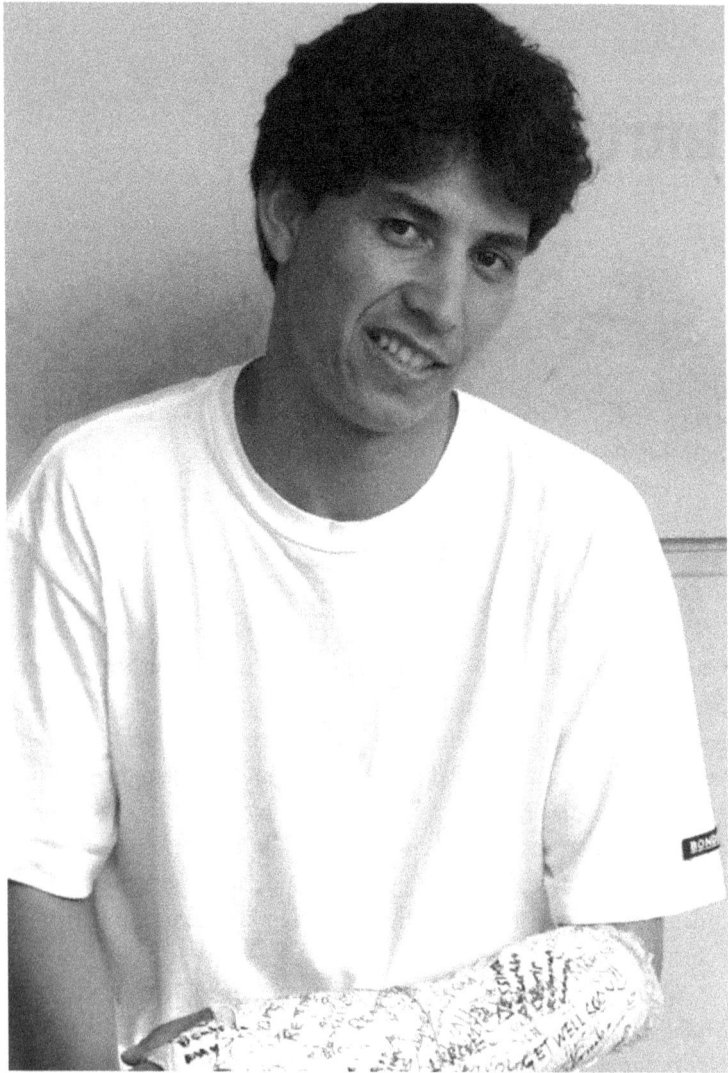
Ali Mullaie on Nauru
Photo: Michael Gordon, courtesy of *The Age*

"The government looks favourably upon Ali as a friend to our people, and appreciates very much the work he has done for our school children. He will be missed as he departs for Australia, but he carries our best wishes and we would welcome his return visit to renew acquaintances and make new friends in Nauru. I have personal confidence Ali will do well in Australia in whichever field he chooses."

At Nauru College, a farewell party was hastily organised and principal Floria Detabene made a generous speech. Her reference told how the school had come to depend on Mullaie to fix its computers, help staff with computer skills and teach students in remedial reading and desktop publishing. He had even become the school's digital photographer for the end-of-year magazine. In performing these duties, she noted that he had never complained about anything and always been punctual. "Mr Ali has become a dear friend to the students and staff of Nauru College. He will be greatly missed."

Shamel Mahmoodi, who ran the processing centre for the International Organisation for Migration, also penned a reference, this one paying tribute to the work Mullaie had done teaching English and computer skills to the other asylum seekers. "As a volunteer, Ali was essentially on call 24 hours a day," he wrote. When he was not teaching, his "linguistic abilities enabled him to interpret for IOM and others in meetings." He also helped in camp management and "provided valuable suggestion for improvement of quality of life in the camps."

All of this was said about a young man whose claim for refugee status was ultimately found to be genuine – someone clearly possessing outstanding qualities, yet also someone the Australian government had been prepared to make an example of in the name of border protection.

For Mullaie, leaving Nauru was considerably less traumatic than arriving in December 2001, or the many times since then when the isolation, uncertainty and memories of past trauma enveloped and very nearly suffocated him. But it was an event tinged with sadness because he was leaving friends who were still waiting for official recognition of their fear of persecution if they returned to their homeland – friends like Arif Hussaini, who had responded to Ali's good news by hugging him warmly, then collapsed when he realised his own Nauru nightmare was not over.

And it was only the beginning of a new chapter of uncertainty for Ali Mullaie. He possessed refugee status but, under Australia's border protection policy, that did not immediately entitle him to permanent protection or the prospect of being reunited with the parents and siblings he had been forced to leave behind.

•

Ali Mullaie's life in offshore detention began in pandemonium. On 8 November 2001 the old Indonesian coastal trader on which he was travelling from Indonesia to Australia was intercepted by the Australian Customs vessel *Arnhem Bay* as it made its way towards Ashmore Reef. Mullaie owed his spot on the boat to Fatima Shahi Husseini, a young, pregnant Afghan woman who was making the trip with her husband, Sayyed. She had intervened when the people smugglers in charge of the vessel told Mullaie and several others they should wait for another boat. She insisted they had paid their money and were accompanying her. Reluctantly, the smuggler acquiesced.

Mullaie was at the front of the crowded vessel when a party from a second vessel, the patrol boat HMAS *Wollongong*, climbed on board. It was then that black smoke began billowing out from the front of the boat, triggering a panic on the deck. Next came an explosion and the instruction from the Navy sailors for all passengers to jump into the sea.

As one of the asylum seekers who were initially refused passage, Mullaie had not been given a life jacket. All he could find on the deck was a jacket designed for a child, torn in half and useless. He then found a plank of wood and weighed up his limited options. A tubby man behind him on the deck warned that he would hurt himself if he jumped in clutching the plank. "Give the wood to me," he suggested, promising he would throw it in after Mullaie was in the water. Mullaie did not trust him. He was almost petrified with fear because he could not swim. So he jumped in, holding the wood, and badly jarred his arm on impact. Then he invited others who were in the water to join him.

Also in the sea was Aslam Kazimi, another young Afghan asylum seeker. During his time in transit in Indonesia, Kazimi had seen a video of the film *Titanic*. As he struggled among the throng of flailing arms and legs, he felt as though he was an extra in the movie's most dramatic scene. It was frightening, but almost surreal. He also remembered how, in the film, passengers dragged each other down attempting to save themselves, so he struggled to find some clear water, away from the others. Kazimi was barely conscious when he was pulled into a rescue boat and taken to the *Wollongong*. The first thing he recalls seeing was the bodies of two women who had drowned despite desperate efforts by crew members to save and revive them. One of them was the young and pregnant Fatima Shahi Husseini. It is among the many scenes Kazimi will never forget.

Ali Mullaie spent almost two hours in the water and was the last asylum seeker to be rescued that day. He had been joined on the plank of wood, to which he was clinging, by four other people, including a young girl who would later become one of his students on Nauru. From time to time in the months ahead on that tiny island state, they would remind each other of their shared experience. One of the four would subsequently return to Afghanistan, one was still on Nauru when he departed, the girl was in Melbourne and the fourth had been accepted by New Zealand. Mullaie had to stay in the water when the others were rescued because there was not enough room on the rescue vessel for him. After he was saved, Mullaie was with Sayyed Husseini when the young farmer was told his wife had drowned. They wept together, and Mullaie remembers an Australian sailor retreating to the upper deck where he, too, broke down, consumed by the tragedy, hiding his tears behind his cap.

News of the deaths reached Australia on the last morning of the 2001 federal election campaign, which had opened five weeks earlier with the accusation that desperate asylum seekers had thrown their children overboard when their boat was intercepted. Evidence had just emerged that this claim was untrue, but it was overshadowed on election eve by reports that the fire on Ali Mullaie's boat had been deliberately lit. As one slur on the character of the asylum seekers was beginning to be discredited, another was capturing the headlines. Much later, investigators would conclude that it was impossible to say whether the fire was deliberately lit and that there was no evidence of a plan among the passengers or the crew to destroy or damage the boat if stopped by Australian authorities.

Ali Mullaie was 18 when he was taken into offshore detention. His command of English was extremely limited and he had no computer skills. His escape from danger in Afghanistan was over, but the next chapter in his short life was about to begin. After spending almost two months on Christmas Island, he was off to Nauru, where more than 1200 asylum seekers were detained in two camps. Conditions were oppressive and outsiders were forbidden from offering assistance or reporting to the outside world who these people were, what were their stories and what was happening to them.

This book is about my contact with Ali Mullaie and many others who were affected by the Australian government's Pacific Solution, the name applied to its response to the problem of unauthorised boat arrivals. It is also about the network of Australian support that conducted a relentless campaign to give these people relief or, at least, a dose of hope. In many cases, it was ordinary Australians who played critical roles in improving the lives of asylum seekers and securing positive outcomes. The campaign began to pay serious dividends after more than four years when, faced with a revolt by moderate Liberals led by Petro Georgiou, John Howard agreed on 17 June 2005 that his policy of mandatory detention should have a "softer edge."

CHAPTER 1

Excuse me, Mr Harris

This policy that collectively punishes people who are themselves
innocent in order to prevent other things occurring is clearly flawed
in international law.

– Paul Komesaroff, Monash Centre for the Study
of Ethics in Medicine and Society

The first time I sought permission to visit the offshore detention centre on Nauru, I went straight to the top. It was early
in March 2002 and Commonwealth leaders had gathered at
a luxury resort at Coolum on the Sunshine Coast in Queensland for
their biennial heads of government meeting. John Howard was the
host and Rene Harris, the president of Nauru, was among those in
attendance. Usually, given the scale of these gatherings and the
massive security presence, there are very few opportunities to
mingle with the leaders. At Coolum, however, the media were
invited to a cocktail party with the prime ministers and presidents
of Commonwealth countries. Harris was among those at the reception.

I had not met the Nauruan president before, but thought a personal approach might just secure me a visa. John Howard's Pacific
Solution had been up and running for only a matter of months,
but already it was clear that journalists were not welcome to visit
the world's smallest nation. The policy began with the decision on

SIEV X survivor Faris Kadhem Shohani and his son Ali
Photo: Simon O'Dwyer, courtesy of *The Age*

27 August 2001 to refuse the Norwegian freighter, the *Tampa*, permission to enter Australia with its cargo of 433 rescued asylum seekers. The aim, as John Howard expressed it, was to send a strong message to people smugglers around the world that Australia was not a "soft touch."

The prime minister had vowed that the *Tampa* would never be permitted to land in Australian waters, but sticking to the commitment meant finding some other place where the human cargo could be unloaded and processed, somewhere where there was no access to the Australian legal system. And it would be better still if there was no scrutiny by the Australian media. What better than a cash-strapped, aid-reliant Pacific state (or states) prepared to perform this service for a fee? As David Adeang would remark much later, the offer made by the Australian government to Harris to set up processing camps on Nauru was "simply too good to refuse".

With me at the cocktail party was Mark Forbes, a colleague at *The Age* who had reported on Pacific affairs for several years and had been to Nauru to cover the Pacific Island Forum just before the *Tampa* incident. "I'll introduce you," he offered. We picked a moment when the president was between conversations, standing with his back against the wall. Mark stretched out his hand. "Excuse me, Mr Harris," he began. "Mark Forbes from *The Age*. Can I introduce you to Michael…" At that moment, Harris abruptly turned his back on us, muttering something about *The Age* and Forbes that conveyed a mixture of antagonism and contempt. There was a faintly comical touch to the gesture, however, as it left Harris facing a blank wall as the cocktail party proceeded around him.

It was only when we returned to the other end of the room that Mark suggested a reason for the president's hostility. "Maybe it's because I recently wrote that his government was corrupt," he said, almost sheepishly. "Oh," I replied. In several articles, Forbes had written about shady dealings on Nauru and extravagance at the top, but Harris had continued to take his calls. Not any more. That was my first and only face-to-face encounter with Harris.

Some time later, I wrote a letter to the Nauruan government requesting a visa. After many phone calls went unanswered and several months passed, I received a brief formal reply. My request had been rejected. No reason was given. When Australia's immigration minister at the time, Philip Ruddock, came to have lunch at *The Age*, I tried again. I put the case for transparency and suggested he might be able to encourage the Nauruan government to at least examine my request. In his sometimes infuriatingly polite way, Ruddock made it clear that he was not going to assist. This was hardly surprising. Although the Howard government always maintained that it was up to Nauru to decide who was allowed access to the asylum seekers, it strongly supported actions that prevented the human consequences of its border protection policy being reported.

The tone had been set in the midst of the children overboard saga in September 2001, the episode that topped and tailed the election campaign. Having demonised asylum seekers as "queue-jumpers" who were prepared to blackmail Australia by throwing their children overboard, the government took steps to ensure that their faces were not shown to the Australian people. As the director-general of Defence public affairs, Brian Humphreys, told the Senate committee investigating the children overboard affair: "We got some guidance ensuring there were no personalising or humanising images taken of SUNCs [suspected unlawful non-citizens]." When Humphreys was pressed on this statement, he agreed with the proposition that "what we have is the Minister for Defence saying in the immediate post-Tampa environment, 'Don't humanise the refugees.'"

The inquiry concluded that the public affairs plan for Operation Relex, the government's post-Tampa border protection regime, had two clear objectives. "The first was to ensure that the Minister [of Defence] retained absolute control over the facts which could and could not become public during the Operation. The second was to ensure that no imagery that could conceivably garner sympathy or cause misgivings about the aggressive new border protection regime would find its way into the public domain."

Faced with the refusal of the Nauruan government to allow media, lawyers and human rights advocates to visit the country, it was not surprising that some journalists and activists resorted to extreme measures to secure access. The human rights advocate and artist, Kate Durham, and a BBC reporter posed as tourists to enter Nauru on a three-day transit permit in 2002. Late in the same year, SBS reporter Bronwyn Adcock used the same technique to report on a riot at one of the two Nauru centres. Adcock managed to get inside the camp by wearing a chador and being mistaken for one of the asylum seekers. The result was an award-winning documentary.

During this period, I interviewed one of the asylum seekers from Nauru at the Maribyrnong immigration detention centre, where he had been transferred for medical treatment. He had been on Nauru since his boat was intercepted at Ashmore Reef ten months earlier. Under the government's post-*Tampa* legislation the young man was classified a "transitory person," with no right to seek an Australian visa. He was among several hundred Afghans who were awaiting a decision on their appeals after their claims for refugee status had been rejected, largely on the basis of the changed circumstances in Afghanistan after the defeat of the Taliban. Almost 240 of them were from the *Tampa*.

Such was his fear of prejudicing his chances that the man asked me not to use his name. But he was forthcoming about his no-win situation. "I'm always thinking if they send me back I will be killed or starve and if I remain for four or five years in detention it will also be difficult. We'll turn crazy," he said.

Twelve months after the *Tampa* incident it seemed clear that the government's policy had achieved its objective. For nine months not a single boat had attempted to bring asylum seekers to Australia. Critics would argue there was a host of explanations for this, including reduced "push" factors in Afghanistan and Iraq, and that the treatment of asylum seekers was not a critical factor. Philip Ruddock, cast within the Liberal Party as the hero of the 2001 election, emphatically disagreed, asserting the government had set "the benchmark when it comes to managing borders."

But the goal was achieved at considerable cost to those who fled persecution, particularly those from Afghanistan and Iraq. The Canberra-based regional representative of the United Nations High Commissioner for Refugees, Michel Gabaudan, remarked that the Australian system of dealing with unauthorised boat arrivals was the most severe in the Western world. "What makes Australia's detention system so invidious is that it combines the three elements of being mandatory, indefinite and non-reviewable," he said.

There were other elements of the policy that made the system even more punitive. Much more. After the *Tampa* was refused entry and before the government went to an election (on the slogan "We decide who comes to this country and the circumstances in which they come"), harsh new conditions were applied to those who had made a successful claim for refugee status and had been released into the community on temporary protection visas. For new arrivals, an offshore processing regime had been introduced.

But the most odious aspect of the system was its basis in the notion of deterrence: that the treatment of one set of people, unau-

thorised arrivals, would deter another set of people – people smugglers or asylum seekers – from attempting to breach Australia's
border protection policy. "This policy that collectively punishes
people who are themselves innocent in order to prevent other
things occurring is clearly flawed in international law," said Paul
Komesaroff, the director of the Monash Centre for the Study of
Ethics in Medicine and Society. "But the other profound implication is the extent to which it is damaging to Australian society to
embed at the level of public policy a practice that is deeply unethi-
cal: punishing individuals in order to achieve an exogenous public
policy objective."

Paris Aristotle, a member of the government's Immigration
Detention Advisory Group and the director of the Victorian Foundation for Survivors of Torture, suggested that, in time, the
government's treatment of those who came by boat would be
likened to the forced removal of indigenous children from their
families. "If you took the characteristics of dispossession, separation, isolation, trauma, complete lack of power over your lives and
a lack of judicial redress, all those elements exist in how we are
dealing with this at this point of time," he said. "I think history will
judge this path very harshly as a result."

Harry Minas, another member of the government's advisory
group and the director of Melbourne University's Centre for International Mental Health, agreed, but suggested it would not take long
before it was recognised that the balance between protecting borders
and human rights had been lost. "I think in a few years we will seriously be wondering what the hell we were doing and what the hell
we were thinking," he told me. "How was it that the very clear advice
about the harmful consequences of treating people in the way that
we're treating them seemed not to make any substantial impact on
either the policy itself or the manner in which the policy was implemented? I don't think that anybody is going to look back on this as
a kind of an example of the best that this country is capable of."

When I put these concerns to Ruddock in August of 2002, he
was unmoved. The psychological damage that came with the

prospect of never being able to have permanency or be reunited with loved ones had to be weighed against "the potential loss of life of encouraging people to get in boats and try and get here." Back then, Ruddock was confident that the situation on Nauru would be resolved fairly quickly once the international community agreed to allow the forced return of those whose claims for refugee status were rejected. The Afghans had been offered a modest financial incentive to return voluntarily and Ruddock was convinced that, once compulsion became a reality, the overwhelming majority of the Afghans would take the money and return of their own volition.

"I think we will find movement on these matters faster rather than later because other countries are now starting to recognise that voluntary returns get you some way, but people won't think realistically about voluntary returns while they know that there is no requirement for forced returns," he said. "Once they know that that situation has been reached, they will tend to accept (relocation) packages."

.

Around the first anniversary of the *Tampa* incident, in August 2002, I interviewed two of the survivors of the SIEV X tragedy that had claimed 353 lives eleven months earlier. SIEV stands for the "suspected illegal entry vessels" intercepted during the government's Operation Relex; SIEV X was a vessel that sank, unrecognised by Australian authorities, on the journey from Indonesia to Australia.

Amal Hassan Basry was one of seven survivors to be offered temporary protection in Australia after being found to be a refugee. The offer was made because she had a family link to this country: her husband, Abbas al-Shiakly, already had a temporary protection visa, or TPV, that was due to expire the following year. At her new home in the Melbourne suburb of Broadmeadows Amal described in near forensic detail how almost 400 people were coerced into boarding a small, unsafe and ill-equipped boat: the trip in five buses with curtains drawn to the apartments where they prepared for the voyage; the demand that the women and children board first, apparently to ensure the men followed; the refusal to return mobile phones surrendered the previous week; the attempt to plug a hole with material from a pair of jeans; the decision of the men not to let it be known that the engine had failed and could not be repaired; the sound of women screaming as the boat sank; the farewell kiss with her teenage son, who also managed to survive; the two mysterious lights in the distance as she clung on to the body of a drowned woman; and, finally, the rescue by Indonesian fishermen alerted when they saw floating luggage and bodies.

After saying all this through an interpreter, Amal looked at me intensely and said in English: "I was like a camera. I remember everything." It was only as I was about to leave that she broke down and cried, explaining that another son was still in Iran and he feared being forcibly returned to Iraq to an uncertain fate.

Six months after she arrived in Melbourne, Amal was confronted with another life and death struggle. She was diagnosed with breast cancer and then bone cancer. In November 2004, while she was receiving treatment in a Melbourne hospital, Amal received a phone call from the immigration department. "Congratulations," the voice said. She had been granted a permanent protection visa and could begin the process of seeking to be reunited with her other son.

The next time I saw Amal was in May 2005 when she spoke at a fundraiser for the Fitzroy Learning Network, one of the main support agencies for refugees in Melbourne. This time she did not need an interpreter and it is safe to say that her courage, conviction and humanity left an enduring impression on those who attended.

•

A few weeks after my first meeting with Amal, the first anniversary of the sinking of SIEV X was marked by a multi-faith memorial service in Reservoir. Faris Fadhil Kadhem Shohani, another SIEV X survivor, was among those who attended. A few days later, I met him at his rented home in Broadmeadows. He spoke with the help of an interpreter while his mother, who had come on an earlier boat with his son Ali, served a stew of lamb and broad beans with rice and bread.

Shohani is an Iraqi Kurd who spent 21 years in Iran as a non-citizen. Now he was having to cope with life as a temporary person. He gave me two reasons for his decision to flee Iran: he feared the man who had given him work at his textile factory was about to be exposed and would face persecution, and he wanted his two children, Ali and Zahra, to be able to attend school, something they could not do in Iran. Shohani travelled with his wife, Leyla, and seven-year-old Zahra. His account was just as detailed and totally consistent with Amal's, but with no happy ending. He even remembered how Zahra kissed the people smuggler Abu Quassey good-bye before they left Sumatra. "Thank you very much. Tomorrow we'll see Ali," she said. Although the vessel seemed hopelessly ill-equipped for the voyage, Quassey exuded confidence. "Be like lions," Faris remembered him declaring. "Don't fear anything. Leave the worry about Indonesian immigration to me."

The first indication of trouble, Shohani recalled, came even before the vessel had made it to the orange buoy that the asylum seekers were told would signal they were in international waters. The captain, an old man, was looking very worried and had only one crew member to assist him, a much younger man. When he asked for those with mechanical skills to help fix the pump, a group that would make the key decisions from that point on came together spontaneously. They included mechanics and electricians, but they were hampered by the lack of tools and spare parts and the fact that the back-up machinery was old, corroded and useless. It was this group of asylum seekers who suggested to the captain that he turn off the engine "to give it a little break".

As the sea became rougher the boat started taking water, panic set in and the decision was taken by those who had assumed leadership to throw the luggage overboard. "Zahra was upset, crying because the toys she was taking to Ali would be lost, even the batteries," Shohani said.

Then came the decision to throw the food and water overboard to further lighten the load. Finally, it was decided that the men should also jump into the sea. When Zahra pleaded with her father to stay, he tried to allay her concern by saying the others would think him lacking in courage if he stayed. "Don't worry what other people say about you," she responded. "I need you." The weather was stormy and he recalled their attempts to attract the attention of a plane they saw by burning clothes that were still dry and waving the flaming garments at the sky.

When the boat sank another twenty centimetres, Shohani said he suggested the three of them jump together, holding hands. While he was trying to reassure his daughter, who could not swim, a wave "like a mountain" hit from the right and the boat capsized, trapping the women and children below deck. In the water, "everybody started to cling to me, and Zahra lost her grip on me and her mum lost her grip on me, and I had to free myself from all these women and children clinging on me and swim towards Leyla, my wife, about five metres away." But, as he was approaching his wife, she shouted, "Why come to me? Go to Zahra." Those would be his wife's last words.

"Zahra was wearing a lifejacket, but the waves kept tossing her and I tried to follow her like a fish. Then it was like when butter melts. She disappeared. I don't know where." Shohani swam back to the others and found Leyla's lifeless body, floating in the water. Hours later, with perhaps 50 survivors still clinging to debris and floating bodies, some wearing lifejackets, Shohani says they saw two ships and a smaller boat. Despite their calls, screams and whistles, they seemed not to be able to attract their attention. Who were they? Was it the failing light that stopped them from responding, or an act of criminal negligence?

Shohani slipped into unconsciousness. He woke the next morning and found himself alone. In a floating black plastic bag, he found some water, apples and biscuits. Then he saw a whale coming towards him. "I said (to myself) I didn't drown and this would finish me off." But it didn't. He endured several more hours, clinging to debris before he became the first survivor to be spotted by Indonesian fishermen who came looking after seeing the floating luggage.

Once on the fishing boat, Shohani remembered retrieving a sodden photograph of his wife and children and explaining that his wife and daughter were gone. "He hug me [and said] 'I sorry, sorry, sorry', he take my clothes, give me bath and new clothes and say 'Relax'." But when Shohani realised they were heading back to Jakarta, he says he screamed that they must look for others. They found another 44.

Back in Jakarta, the survivors were processed quickly by the United Nations High Commissioner for Refugees. All but nine were found to be refugees. Most were accepted by Scandinavian countries and offered permanent residency. The seven who had relatives in Australia were told they had been accepted as refugees and given five-year temporary protection visas. This class of visa was introduced in 1999 and toughened in 2001 to deter people from using people smugglers. Although accepted as refugees, TPV-holders had no permanency, could not leave Australia to visit relatives and expect to return, had no right of reunion with immediate family members outside Australia, and had limited access to support services, including English-language training.

It was nine months before Shohani was reunited with Ali, his son, who had arrived safely and spent six months in the Woomera detention centre with his grandmother before being found to be a refugee and given a three-year TPV. He was in grade four at a Broadmeadows primary school.

As I left his home, Shohani seemed unburdened by telling his story, but made no attempt to camouflage his anxiety about the future. "I spent all my life without citizenship and now I am offered temporary residency," he said. "I have no hope, no future, because my situation is now similar to my past back in Iran. I am not settled. I belong nowhere."

•

More than two and a half years after our first meeting and almost four years after the tragedy, I went back to see Shohani and his family. He had remarried and there was no need for an interpreter this time. A few weeks earlier, he had been granted permanency, along with his mother and son. Ali was now "an Aussie," he told me, with genuine pride. While it was quickly clear that he had made great progress since our first meeting and was delighted that Ali was doing well at school, he remained haunted by the sinking of the boat known as SIEV X.

In April 2005, he had been called to give evidence in Brisbane against Khaleed Daoed, an alleged co-organiser of the voyage, who was facing twelve charges of people smuggling and up to twenty years in jail. Shohani was pleased that Daoed had been charged – he was subsequently found guilty – but he considered this a minor issue when compared with the questions that kept coming back to him.

"You want to show me Khaleed?" he recalled asking from the witness box. "Yes, this is Khaleed, 100 per cent this is Khaleed. He is smuggler and he is criminal. But why you no ask me about this boat in the night [that] no come help us? Why you no ask me about this airplane before my boat sink in the ocean? Why you no ask me about this?" No one offered an answer. "Everyone keep silent."

Achieving permanent residency had lifted one source of anxiety, but it was insignificant when compared with the horrors that returned in his dreams and even during his twelve-hour shifts at a meat works.

"Sometimes, I'm in the work in factory, sometimes [it is] like a film in front of me, like cinema. I see in the front [of me], God, I see my daughter, [saying] come help me. I see my wife. She is screaming, 'Faris, take my daughter bring for me'. After three minutes all finished, my daughter and my wife. But after three minutes, I see a lot, a lot [more]. I see women, men, boys, girls. All gone. Yes, too much. Sometimes [at work] I talk a lot, I screaming, someone says 'Faris. What I do for you? Why you screaming?' I say, 'I sorry, I'm with myself.'"

As we sipped tea and ate cake, the conversation shifted to the happier subject of Ali, who was now in year six at primary school. Ali said he wanted to be a mechanic, nominated maths and science as his favourite subjects and talked with passion about his love of playing soccer and watching Australian Rules football. He barracked for the Brisbane Lions. Jonathan Brown was his favourite player. When, much later, Shohani returned the conversation to SIEV X and the unanswered questions, there was a calm in his voice. "One day the truth will come," he said with certainty.

Ali Sarwari at work in Melbourne
Photo: James Boddington, courtesy of *The Age*

CHAPTER 2

The Kiwi way

*It's ridiculous that we can turn away people of this quality and it's
ridiculous that he should be separated from his family. I'm just
stonkered by it. It's beyond belief.*

— BOBBY CINCOTTA, MELBOURNE RESIDENT

L ike many Australians, Jeanie Gibb was outraged by the
Tampa episode and keen to do something, anything, to assist
those facing years of uncertainty and separation under the
Howard government's border protection policy. Her opportunity
came early in 2003 when she heard Anne Horrigan-Dixon give a
lunch-time talk on how the Fitzroy Learning Network was assisting
refugees who had been released from detention on temporary protection visas. Horrigan-Dixon recalled the day a group of Afghans
knocked on her door at the centre requesting help with their
English and captivated her audience with stories about these
remarkable, resilient, but terribly sad people. After the talk, Gibb
was among several women who approached Horrigan-Dixon
wanting to know more. She was invited to a party for the refugees
at the centre the following week.

At the party, the former teacher struck up a conversation with
Ali Sarwari, who had arrived in Australia on 26 January 2000. After
spending seven months in the Woomera detention centre and being
found to be a refugee, Sarwari was released into the community on
a temporary protection visa. He had fled Afghanistan after his

father was murdered by the Taliban and he had been arrested, beaten and interrogated. He managed to escape after his father-in-law bribed two members of the Taliban secret police. When Gibb asked about his family, she was shocked by the response. His mother was still in Afghanistan, caring for his young son. His wife, daughter and brother were all in detention on Nauru, having suffered further persecution after his departure and been forced to attempt to follow him to Australia.

Sarwari discovered that the three were on Nauru when his brother, Sajjad, wrote to the Association of Hazaras of Victoria seeking news of Sarwari. The letter reached Mohammad Arif, the association's public affairs officer, who in a neat coincidence shared a flat with Ali Sarwari and was his best friend.

"I'll never forget that party at the Fitzroy Learning Network," Gibb told me much later. "He cried and I cried, and I recall saying to Ali: 'I don't know what I'm going to do or how I'm going to do it, but I'm going to get your family back together.'"

From that night, Sarwari would visit Gibb at her Malvern home each weekend. She helped with his English and letter-writing and became his principal support in the mainstream community. It was Gibb who wrote to the office of the Australian Democrats senator Andrew Bartlett, who was organising his own visit to Nauru. She told Bartlett that Sarwari was working as a tiler and stone mason and feared for the safety of his family if they were forced to return to Afghanistan. He was desperate for them to be reunited and was earning more than enough money to support them. The letter concluded: "If Ali is considered to be a refugee (even only a temporary one) then surely his wife and little daughter should also be! As a teacher with over 30 years experience in dealing with young children, I hate to imagine the harm being done to [Ali's daughter] little Sakina and all the other children in detention. It is a national disgrace!"

Gibb also wrote of Sarwari's pain: "He is suffering so much. He lives day and night with the uncertainty of his life as a temporary person and the horror of his family's cruel detention and his separation from them. I see at first hand his despair and anguish, and I never cease to be inspired by the courage, determination and strength of character of this kind, caring, gentle man."

As it turned out, the Sarwaris were one of many families separated by the Howard government's Pacific Solution. In nine cases, one parent was recognised as a refugee and living in the community on a temporary protection visa, while the other parent and the children were in detention on Nauru. In several other cases, the father was in Australia and the wife and children were in Indonesia and Jordan, having been recognised as refugees. Five such families remained separated in July 2005.

The decision to deny any guarantee of permanent settlement and family reunions to refugees who came, unauthorised, by boat was taken in 1999, almost two years before the *Tampa* episode. It reflected the intention to deter people from using people smugglers. As the immigration minister, Philip Ruddock, explained:

Since 1994, when immediate access to permanent residence was introduced for refugees in Australia, the commercial saleability of Australia as smuggling destination has been very high. Permanent residence and the family reunion rights that flow from it are clearly a major attraction.

The real question we must ask ourselves is whether we are prepared to stand by while smugglers arrange for Australia's resettlement contribution to be taken up by people who select themselves or whether we should try to retain those places for those in most need.

The decision to provide unauthorised arrivals found to be refugees with access to temporary residence only in the first instance is fully consistent with our fundamental obligations towards refugees.

It provides them with the protection required under the Refugees Convention. They have work rights, access to special benefit and are able to gain access to Medicare. They can apply for protection again and, if found to still need protection after 30 months, are then eligible for permanent residence.

For those who enter lawfully and seek refugee protection, Australia continues to be more generous than the Refugees Convention requires by providing immediate access to permanent residence to those found to be refugees.

Treating refugees differently depending on whether they arrive lawfully or unlawfully does not mean we are penalising unauthorised arrivals. What it does mean is that we are being more generous in cases where people play by the rules of the international protection arrangements and where they comply with Australia's laws.

Undeniably, however, unauthorised arrivals *were* being penalised. They were being denied rights Australia had, until this point, afforded those who came to these shores and were found to be in need of protection. In a response that was indicative of Labor's failure to put principle before politics on the question of refugees, the Opposition's immigration spokesman at the time, Con Sciacca, remarked that although Labor did not believe the measures would work, the party did not want to be blamed for the problem of people smuggling. "This was essentially a vote against queue-jumping," he said. "My colleagues decided Labor could not in conscience support a situation where people who come here illegally get the same treatment as people who arrive through proper processes."

After the *Tampa*, a harsh system for dealing with unauthorised arrivals was made even tougher. Those who transited for at least seven days in a country where they could have sought and obtained protection were told they would never be able to access a permanent visa and never have family reunion rights in Australia.

While the impact of the 2001 measures in stopping the people smuggling trade is open to debate, what is clear is that the 1999 decision to prevent family reunions failed to have the desired effect. Refugee advocates had warned that it would actually encourage women and children to undertake hazardous voyages because they would see this as the only way of being reunited with husbands who came earlier and were found to have legitimate claims to protection. This is precisely what happened.

When Ed Killesteyn, a senior department official, appeared before a Senate committee in August of 2002, he was asked why it was that children were arriving in family groups more often than two years earlier. "I do not know about the statistics," he replied, "but certainly we would agree with that particular trend. Essentially it arises as a consequence of the inability of those people who are granted asylum in Australia, or have been hitherto granted asylum through the temporary protection visa arrangements, to subsequently apply to bring their family to Australia. I suspect it is a direct consequence of the entitlements that temporary protection visa holders have in terms of family migration."

Andrew Bartlett made his first visit to Nauru in June 2003 and was deeply affected by the emotional state of the detainees, particularly the women and children whose husbands were in Australia. "It's hard to know which are more distressed: the kids and wives on Nauru, stuck in the middle of nowhere being pressured to go back to the place they fled, or the husbands, stuck here and separated from their loved ones for almost three years," he told me. "The trauma they are going through is just indescribable." His most awkward moment was trying to explain to Sarwari's six-year-old daughter why she could not see her father. "It's hard enough explaining something to a kid when there's a logical reason. The complete absurdity of it just added to the horror of it all." At the time, there were some 353 asylum seekers in the two camps on Nauru and Bartlett was assured they had all been rejected and had "no realistic durable solution option other than assisted voluntary return."

Bartlett raised the issue of the separated families with the Canberra office of the United Nations High Commissioner for Refugees. So did Rashida Joseph, who had been working as a support worker for refugees on temporary protection visas in Brisbane. She was particularly concerned about Ahmad al-Aridhi, an Iraqi man whose wife and daughter were on Nauru.

The UNHCR's Michel Gabaudan made it plain on several occasions that the practice of denying refugee status to the immediate family of those whose refugee claims had been accepted was contrary to the UNHCR Handbook on Procedures and Criteria for Determining Refugee Status. In a submission to the Senate's legal and constitutional committee, the UNHCR said:

> The unity of the family members is a fundamental human right, and the impact of transfer of asylum seekers to third countries upon this right is of grave concern. This right includes maintaining family unity for members arriving in Australian territory together, as well as assuring family reunion for members arriving separately. When coupled with the use of temporary protection visas by Australia, which do not provide for family reunion as a basic individual right, the impact of such State action may result in a breach of Australia's formal obligations under various human rights instruments, including the Convention on the Rights of the Child, as well as ignoring standards that Australia has helped create and promote.

The day Gabaudan appeared before the committee, in early August 2002, he gave a "practical example" of the UNHCR's policy on derivative status:

> You have a man who has political opinions in a country where this is severely discriminated against, who escapes so as not to be jailed or tortured or whatever. His wife may not know anything about his activities but that does not give the international community the right to separate them forever, and that is why we consider that his family should be reunited with him.

But the UNHCR handbook provided no comfort for Sediqa Sarwari or the other wives on Nauru. Under pressure to take a modest financial incentive and return to Afghanistan or Iraq, they were given a set of answers to questions that served only to aggravate their feeling of hopelessness and desperation. Consider these two examples:

Question 7: My application for refugee status was refused but my husband is in Australia. Why can't I join him?

Each case is assessed on its merits. Your claims have been assessed separately from your husband's claims, because you travelled at different times. The refugee determination process on your claims is now finalised. Under the conditions of your husband's stay in Australia, he is not able to sponsor you. Like all refused asylum seekers you cannot remain in Nauru indefinitely. You should consider voluntary repatriation now.

The answer did not say it, but there was only one conclusion to draw: if you wanted to be reunited with your husband, whose fear of persecution if he returned had been judged to be well-founded, your only choice was to return and to convince him to leave Australia and confront the very danger he had fled.

Then there was question 8:

Can I stay on Nauru?

No. The Australian Government has a memorandum of understanding with the Government of Nauru which states that all asylum seekers will be processed as quickly as possible and either resettled or returned within a reasonable time frame. You may not stay on Nauru indefinitely and there is no chance of you going to Australia by staying here longer.

We are all currently focussing on voluntary repatriation and encourage you to sign the IOM (International Organisation for Migration) voluntary return forms. Two million people have returned to Afghanistan in the last 12 months. There is a strong interest in return within the Iraqi group. The agreement with the Government of Nauru is that no asylum seekers will remain on Nauru. Your best interests are served by assisting IOM in identifying a solution to your individual circumstances. The Australian

Government is exploring all options for return including involuntary return.

There, in the final sentence, was the threat: if you don't depart of your own volition, you will be forcibly removed.

•

By the middle of 2003, Jeanie Gibb was not alone in being concerned about the welfare of the separated families. Jawed Ali was another of the men separated from their wives and children, but his condition was far more acute than the rest. In May, the Canberra migration agent Marion Le was alerted by Diana Davison-Mowle, a resident of the New South Wales country town of Young, that Ali was being treated at the Sunshine Adult Acute Psychiatry Unit after attempting suicide.

Davison-Mowle had met Jawed and another Afghan refugee at a supermarket in Young and offered them help. He replied that he would be grateful for some assistance with his English and, over the next few months, she became "extraordinarily committed to these beautiful people."

She was not alone. At the Young meatworks, Jawed, 33, so impressed his fellow workers that when they discovered his wife, Latifa, and daughter, Firsht, were in detention on Nauru, all those on the beef floor signed a statement demanding the family be reunited. It was never made public, says Tony Hewson, former mayor of Young and human resources manager at the abattoir at the time, because of concern that it would make the Howard government less sympathetic to Jawed Ali's case. When I interviewed Hewson late in 2003, he described Jawed as "just one of the best workers we ever had, an amazing guy with a great work ethic and a will to learn."

Jawed had fled Afghanistan after the death of his older brother, who had been interrogated by the Taliban at the family home, taken away, tortured and murdered, his body paraded in their village. His father, who had been prominent in the resistance, had already been killed fighting against the Taliban. The Taliban were convinced his father had hidden weapons and were determined to either find them or exact retribution, or both. Ali's mother urged him, as the next most obvious target, to escape.

In a statement prepared with the help of a migration agent at the Curtin detention centre, Jawed told of his fears for the welfare of his family. "I have been very much affected by my experiences with the Taliban. I still have terrible nightmares about the time they came to our house, and sometimes I wake up sweating." Released after eight months at Curtin, he sought work, first in Brisbane, and then in Sydney.

In the early months, he was racked by guilt because he could not find a job and send home money to provide for his family. That changed when he went to Young, where work was available at the meatworks. After several attempts to make contact with his family through Red Cross, Jawed was told his wife was on Nauru. In a letter, she explained that his mother and his two sons, Abass and Asid, had been killed, his younger sister and brother were missing, believed dead, and his daughter, two months old when he fled, was alive and with her mother.

In the months that followed, Jawed witnessed from a distance the deterioration of his wife's mental and physical health on Nauru. He began suffering from depression. In 2002, he came to Melbourne, found work and met Emily Williams, a voluntary English tutor with SPAN Community House. "He would come to class during Ramadan, having had no food and worked all day, with pages and pages of words and questions about learning English," Williams recalled. "I was just astonished at the amount of work he would put in."

Jawed's depression intensified around April after letters confirming his wife's and daughter's deterioration on Nauru. As he told me: "I think, why they not dying in Afghanistan? They die quicker. Why I not dying in Afghanistan with my brother?" One night, consumed by grief, he wandered into the traffic, hoping to be run over. "I couldn't control myself," he said. Eventually he was taken to a police station, where he pleaded to be shot. There was no shortage of help from committed agencies but with no prospect of reunion with his wife, and no future, the task of psychologist Conrad Aikin, from Foundation House, and social worker Sarah Kewming was difficult. "The only therapeutic goal we could have with this guy was survival, to keep him alive, day to day," said Aikin.

Meanwhile, on Nauru, the condition of Latifa was deteriorating. In one letter to Le, she wrote of her daughter's joy at finally having a photograph of her father, but her inability to comprehend why they could not be together. The letter concluded: "Please I have one hope in all my life and it is that I be success to be together with my husband."

Early in November, some five months after Le wrote to Ruddock pressing him to reunite Jawed Ali and his wife and daughter "as a matter of urgency," I received news of a breakthrough in the case of the separated families. New Zealand had agreed, in the first instance, to take three of the most desperate cases. Two of the husbands, Jawed Ali and Ali Sarwari, were in Melbourne. The other was an Iraqi man in Brisbane, Ahmad al-Aridhi. Ultimately, the New Zealand government of Helen Clark would reunite all the separated families in cases where the wives and children were on Nauru.

That afternoon I met Jawed Ali at his Preston home after he finished work as a cabinet maker. Sitting on the floor of a room that had only a thin mattress as furniture, he told me his story. When I returned to the office, I rang Gabaudan, who always chose his words with great care when it came to commenting on Australia's border protection policy. It was time to show some compassion, he said. "Two years in detention on Nauru is just a bit too much when your husband is recognised to have a valid refugee claim. These are not people abusing [the system]. They are families who want to be together and this is a very basic human desire."

That weekend, I visited Ali Sarwari where he lived on the thirteenth floor of one of the old housing commission blocks of flats in the inner Melbourne suburb of Fitzroy. He was excited by the prospect of finally being reunited with Sediqa and Sakina, but worried about his younger brother, Sajjad, who had cared for his wife and daughter since their departure from Afghanistan. He was also concerned to do the right thing by his employer, Premier Pools and Spas, and keen to ensure that the job he was working on, a massive suburban pool in Donvale, was finished before he left for New Zealand.

My interview with Sarwari was published on the front page of *The Age* on the following Monday with a picture of Ali working in the pool. His boss, Joe Lazar, described him as the best worker, in terms of craftsmanship and character, he had ever employed. It would take six months of training to bring a qualified tiler up to his standard, he said. But it was Bobby Cincotta, whose pool was being built by Sarwari, who captured the sense of disbelief that Australia was forcing a person of such talent and quality, and a genuine refugee, to leave so that he could be with his family. "It's ridiculous that we can turn away people of this quality and it's ridiculous that he should be separated from his family. I'm just stonkered by it. It's beyond belief."

Among those who were prompted to write to the newspaper about the story was that icon of popular culture, Ian "Molly" Meldrum, who remarked that, as well as his "incredible" craftsmanship, using traditional tools to cut marble, "he is one of the nicest and kindest gentlemen you could ever meet." He went on: "What he and his family went through in Afghanistan was horrendous. And I, as a proud Australian feel angry that our government cannot understand, for a start, their situation and cannot show the compassion to deal with such an extraordinary human struggle for these people just to be decent human beings and get on with their lives."

•

Four months after Jawed Ali and Ali Sarwari left Melbourne, I went to New Zealand to see how they were settling in and witness the very different approach of the New Zealand government to those who were rescued by the *Tampa*. While Australia had gone to extraordinary lengths to keep families apart, lest the hint of a green light be given to the people smugglers, New Zealand had gone to even more trouble to bring them together.

Back in 2001, New Zealand had taken 131 of the 433 asylum seekers who were rescued by the *Tampa*, about forty of them unaccompanied boys. Subsequently, it had quietly taken another 270 from Australia's offshore processing centres on Nauru and Papua New Guinea's Manus Island. Most remarkably, it had undertaken what Qemaji Murati, the acting manager of New Zealand's refugee quota branch, called one of the most ambitious, challenging and delicate family reunion projects ever undertaken by that country. With the help of the UNHCR and the IOM, teams went to Afghanistan, Iraq, Pakistan and Iran, tracked down the families of the refugees and offered them permanent resettlement.

My visit coincided with the arrival of the families of eleven of the *Tampa* boys in Auckland, but first I visited Bushra al-Aridhi, her husband Ahmad and daughter Hawra in Wellington and the Afghan families in Hamilton. Bushra was pregnant and planned to dedicate the birth to the UNHCR official who presented her case to the New Zealand government, Susan Harris-Rimmer. A healthy girl was born a few months later.

Back in Australia, Ahmad had not wanted to speak to me until he was with his wife and daughter. He feared any contact that might jeopardise the reunion. Now he was more than happy to discuss his flight from Saddam Hussein's regime and the trauma of standing by, helpless, as his wife's emotional state deteriorated on Nauru. As we sipped tea, the couple showed me pictures taken on Nauru that captured Bushra's despair. One showed her sitting in the dirt in an extremely distressed state, pleading for help, with six-year-old Hawra trying to comfort her. Another showed security guards preventing the asylum seekers from leaving the camp through the front gate. While the couple spoke with optimism about the family's future in New Zealand, Bushra was concerned for those who remained in island detention. "Please, finish the jail," she said.

At Hamilton, I visited Jawed Ali and his wife and daughter, and also the Sarwari family, who had been joined by Ali's brother Sajjad.

Passionate and energetic, Sajjad expressed grave concern for the others on Nauru and for those who had taken the option of voluntary return.

After a traditional Afghan dinner, Jawed explained how he and Latifa had come to terms with their grief in the weeks after their reunion and resolved to look forward. "We knew that too much thinking about that [the past] was bad [and] that if I continue this, my daughter's future can be dark."

The following day, dozens of Afghan families were reunited at Auckland Airport and at the nearby Mangere refugee reception centre. As we waited for the arrivals to clear customs, one young man confided to me his fear that his little brothers may not recognise him. He need not have worried. They were like peas in a pod. During a welcome ceremony, they were addressed by Ruud Lubbers, the United Nations High Commissioner for Refugees, who recalled hearing the "awful story" that the Australian government had rejected the refugee claims of those who were rescued by the *Tampa*.

"It's a miracle that you survived and then were welcomed here in New Zealand," he said, adding that he would try again to persuade Australian authorities to release the 267 asylum seekers still on Nauru. The response from Immigration Minister Amanda Vanstone was swift and blunt. "That won't be happening," she said. "The offshore processing is the single most effective deterrent to people smugglers."

World Vision's Tim Costello with Amin Jan Amin
Photo: Michael Clayton-Jones, courtesy of *The Age*

CHAPTER 3

When all else fails

It was not good to hurt my body, but I was compelled to do this.

— AMIN JAN AMIN, HUNGER STRIKER
WHO SEWED HIS LIPS TOGETHER ON NAURU

While the Howard government maintained pressure on the Nauru asylum seekers to voluntarily return to their homeland, two trends were becoming apparent. The first was that asylum seekers assessed on the mainland were being treated differently from, and more generously than, those on Nauru. The second was that the situation on the ground in Afghanistan was deteriorating dramatically, with mounting evidence that forced returns were out of the question, at least for the foreseeable future. The dangerous situation was being relayed by some who had accepted the voluntary return package to their friends on Nauru. It was underscored in mid-November 2003 when the first United Nations foreign aid worker was slain by Taliban militants.

Against this background, several of the Afghans on Nauru began a hunger strike, four of them marking World Human Rights Day on 10 December 2003 by stitching their lips together. One of the four was Amin Jan Amin, who had been forced to leave his wife and five children in June 2001. His claim to have been a Christian who had worked for the United Nations and World Vision, and therefore a target for persecution, had not been investigated by those assessing his bid for refugee status, which had been rejected twice. "It was not good to hurt my body, but I was compelled to do this because every night I could not sleep," he told me months later. "I was missing my children, my wife."

The immigration minister, Amanda Vanstone, who had succeeded Ruddock in the portfolio three months earlier, told the protesters to end their "voluntary starvation" and follow the lead of those who had agreed to return to Afghanistan. "The protesters are not refugees," she said. "They have been assessed by either the United Nations High Commissioner for Refugees, or under UNHCR guidelines [by Vanstone's department], not to be refugees. Four hundred and twenty Afghans have already returned home, all with financial assistance. Nineteen returned on 1 December 2003."

But behind the scenes, note *was* being taken of the changed situation in Afghanistan. Within a week of Vanstone's media release, on Christmas Eve, the UNHCR announced that, in the light of new information, it intended to review the cases of many of the 22 Afghans it had previously found not to be refugees. Vanstone responded the same day, saying that as soon as the UNHCR had completed an assessment of those areas where the situation had changed, the government would examine the implications for its caseload on Nauru.

It was another week before Amin Jan Amin took the stitches out of his lips and the others followed his example. The trigger was not the review of the security situation in Afghanistan, but news that his original claims had been examined and found to be legitimate. It was Elaine Smith, a country pharmacist who corresponded with many of the Nauru asylum seekers, and Robyn Evans, a former World Vision employee, who alerted World Vision Australia to Amin's claim to have worked for the organisation in Afghanistan. World Vision's Bill Walker discovered there was a report on the project in question and faxed a letter urging Amin to end the hunger strike so that he could answer questions about the project. Walker said he had approached Marion Le and she was willing to assist in any way "but only if you cease your hunger strike." Amin agreed and, as Walker put it, "it was clear very quickly that he was who he said he was."

One consequence of the protest was that Marion Le was issued with a visa to visit Nauru and represent the asylum seekers. Le had just been awarded the 2003 Human Rights Medal by the Human Rights and Equal Opportunity Commission for her contribution over three decades to advancing human rights. She had opposed the protest from the outset, aware that the UNHCR was in the process of changing its attitude in response to the worsening situation in Afghanistan. In a letter to Vanstone on 10 December, two days after the protest ended, she said the paramount concern of those who had been involved in the protest had not been the adequacy of medical or other services on the Nauru camp, as had been suggested, but "their continued fears of returning to Aghanistan – fears which they maintain are well-founded." On the case of Amin, she wrote:

> I do think that it would be useful for the DIMIA [the Australian Department of Immigration and Multicultural and Indigenous Affairs] to process Mr Amin's case as a matter of urgency, not because he sewed his lips and went on a hunger strike but because he has a compelling case for protection.
>
> The prompt recognition of this fact would go a long way to convincing the detainees on Nauru that the DIMIA is acting in accordance with your Press Release of 24 December and other statements since. It will alleviate some of their immediate concerns that the DIMIA caseload will not be treated fairly.

A more comprehensive submission was sent the following day, pointing out that Amin had given the immigration department his World Vision and UN identity cards, his Christianity baptism certificate and a duplicate of his Afghan passport. It warned: "Given the degree of the current Taliban activity in the Paktia area [where Amin lived] and the general support for the Taliban from the Pashtuns, there is no way for the applicant to escape notice if he returned to the area."

Bill Walker, meanwhile, gathered more information supporting Amin's account, resulting in this letter from Tim Costello to Vanstone on 1 March 2004, the day he became the organisation's chief executive officer.

I am writing to you regarding Mr Amin Jan Amin, who has been detained on Nauru Island for two years.

Amin Jan Amin has been claiming since his arrival that he was formerly employed by World Vision in Afghanistan, Indeed, we have been able to confirm his identity and he is remembered fondly for his behaviour and good work by our former manager of the AusAid funded de-mining program.

We now understand that he has recently been re-interviewed by DIMIA officers and that his claim is being reconsidered.

We are keenly aware that both current and former NGO and UN workers in Afghanistan are being targeted, and in a continuing series of instances killed, by the Taliban. It is clear that there is a high degree of danger, not only for him if he were forced to return, but also for his family in remaining in that part of the world.

In view of his circumstances, we trust that he will be granted refugee status and a permanent protection visa so that he can seek out and if successful bring his wife and children to Australia and be re-united with them. We strongly urge that, in the event he is successful with his claim for refugee status, you also grant him a permanent protection visa.

Based on very positive reports from World Vision staff who supervised him as a World Vision employee in Afghanistan and have since been solicitous of his welfare, we conclude from his work performance, character and abilities, that Amin Jan Amin would make a positive contribution to our country.

Thank you for your consideration of this sensitive issue.

It was several months before Amin was granted a temporary protection visa. When we met in the middle of 2004 after his arrival in Melbourne, two things struck me about him: his hunger for work and his lack of bitterness over the handling of his case. At the time of writing, a year later, he was still waiting to find out whether he had been granted permanent protection and could begin the process of being reunited with his family.

Le's first visit to Nauru convinced her that serious mistakes had been made in handling the claims for refugee status of many of those who remained. She considered that the overwhelming majority were indeed legitimate refugees. She was also struck by one of the detainees who seemed to be constantly busy, always looking after the needs of others. His name was Ali Mullaie. "He seemed to me to be acting like the mother and father and the big sister and brother all rolled into one," Le recalled. "I remember the night before I was leaving, saying to him: 'Ali, does anyone look after you? You're running around looking after everyone. Can I do anything for you?'" she says. "And he said, 'Can you just put your arms around me like a mum?' So I gave him a hug and he absolutely disintegrated. For half an hour he just cried. Then he told me how hard it was to hold himself together every day when he doesn't know where his parents were, and how he worried about a missing brother."

The review by the UNHCR of its remaining Afghan caseload on Nauru was unequivocal. All 22, including the last of those who arrived on the *Tampa*, were declared refugees. Of the immigration department's Afghan caseload of 175 on Nauru, 146 were found to be refugees; the remaining 29 had their claims rejected. Among those who were rejected were Ali Mullaie, Aslam Kazimi and Zahir Dulat Shahi, who expressed his sense of devastation in a letter to an Australian friend, Ben Habib:

Often I think the world is devoid of even the slightest sense of humanity, because there is no place on the planet for me to live freely. How long I should be incarcerated in the trap of those rulers who pretend them self as protector of human rights and democracy on the world, but they denied our rights and treated us brutally and aggressively.

Because I am human being some time the pressure become too much for me to bear and I tell myself I should left this world. How long I should be fettered in the cage and deprived of my own rights? What is my guilt except I sought asylum from brutal and dictatorial regime?

The 168 reassessed by the UNHCR and the Australian immigration department and found to be refugees were resettled in Australia and other countries. By this stage, of the Afghans who had been taken to Nauru, 420 had returned to Afghanistan (many of them reluctantly accepting the government's repatriation package with cash assistance of $2000 per individual and up to $10,000 per family), 309 had been resettled as refugees, 27 had been resettled as humanitarian cases, and one had died. Despite the message that the *Tampa* people would never be allowed to set foot on Australian soil, many were now in the process of starting new lives in Australia.

Sajjad Sarwari kept in touch with many of those who returned and told me the news was not good. Their fears for their safety if they returned to Afghanistan were, indeed, well-founded. Of those he knew, all had now fled to Pakistan or Iran.

·

Ali Reza Irfani's experience upon returning to Afghanistan is typical of many, but his situation is particularly tragic. He arrived on Christmas Island with his wife Fatima and three small children just after the post-*Tampa* decision to excise the island from Australia's migration zone. The decision denied those whose claims were initially rejected any resort to a review tribunal or the courts. Fatima was 29 and still breastfeeding their youngest child.

They had fled their home after Ali Reza, a Hazara and Shiite Muslim, was arrested by the Taliban and threatened with violence for teaching the "wrong" Islamic religion at his school. Their claim for refugee status was rejected and they had 28 days to decide whether or not to accept the $10,000 incentive from the Australian government to go back to Afghanistan. As Ali Reza explained in a written statement:

We were told if we didn't agree to go back to Afghanistan we would be sent to Nauru, which was our worst fear. During this time when we had to make the decision, Fatima cried a lot. In the end we decided to return to Afghanistan even though we were fearful and did not know what we were going back to. The other choice for us was to stay in detention indefinitely which was bad for our children and made me feel mentally disturbed. In the second week of January 2003 we signed papers from DIMIA to say we would return to Afghanistan.

Fatima Irfani's health had worsened over the months they spent in offshore detention and, around June 2002, she was diagnosed with high blood pressure. On 12 January 2003, the week they decided to take their chances and return to Afghanistan, she awoke several times during the night, complaining of headaches. Three days later she went to the Christmas Island hospital and was given non-prescription medicine for the pain and told to rest. The following morning, she collapsed and, after being taken to the local hospital, was flown to Perth.

Judith Quinlivan, a lawyer who had made friends with the family on Christmas Island, attempted to comfort Ali Reza at Perth's Sir Charles Gardiner Hospital, where doctors were fighting to save his wife's life. Quinlivan was refused entry by a guard from the firm that was managing detainees on Christmas Island and told she would have to get approval from the immigration department in Canberra. It took some time to make contact with the relevant official and her request was refused. Quinlivan says she stressed that she had known the family for nearly a year and believed Ali Reza would appreciate seeing a familiar face, but it made no difference. "I stumbled out of the hospital crying with rage and frustration and not being able to comprehend the indignity and inhumanity of our government's position," she later wrote. Ali Reza later told her he had wanted her to be with him and Fatima, and when this was forbidden his heart became so swollen he felt it would burst through his mouth. In a statement signed on 14 February, Reza said he had asked if he could go to see Quinlivan, but was told he could not leave the intensive care unit or make a phone call "and they were the orders of the minister, Mr Ruddock."

Fatima died on 17 January. Her husband and children, who had been flown to Perth to be near their mother, were returned to Christmas Island the following day. Reza agreed to be returned to Afghanistan within weeks, hoping his wife could be buried in their village of Zirak in the province of Ghazni. In an email to supporters, he said he would always remember "the very kind people in Australia." He has kept in contact with Quinlivan and his first email explained how they ended up in Pakistan. In Dubai, Fatima's mother and brothers told him it was unsafe to return to Afghanistan. He also learned that his uncle had recently been killed by the Taliban. "In this situation I had to choose Pakistan, so I travelled from Kabul to Quetta carrying Fatima's body and three children. This journey took about forty hours by van." Fatima was buried in Quetta on 22 February.

In an email dated 15 August 2003, Reza said he felt he had made the right decision to return "because of Fatima's body and the children's future." But he also said that, if he had been alone, he would never have gone back. He was still grieving over Fatima's death and said that "if she had got proper care I think she was still with us and children were still have their mum." Almost a year later, he wrote that he had travelled with the family to Iran but found it impossible to live there because Afghans were routinely deported and they were not "free in the city." It was not safe in Quetta, either, where the law and order situation was terrible and Hazaras were threatened, but he had re-married (his new wife had also lost her spouse) and it was good that his children had someone else to take care of them. He closed by saying he had heard some good news from Nauru, that many had finally been accepted as refugees, including his friend Sayed Shahi. "They are free now, if it is true, so it is very good and I am very pleased for them."

•

In September 2004, the Edmund Rice Centre for Justice published *Deported To Danger*, a study of forty rejected asylum seekers who had tried to convince the Australian government they would not be safe if they were rejected. Only five were found to be "safe for the longer term." One of those interviewed was Rajab, a young Afghan who was rescued by the *Tampa* and taken to Nauru. He complained of the lack of access to legal advice, the poor translations and the pressure to return to Afghanistan, saying he suffered depression, isolation and uncertainty. It was impossible for Rajab and his companions to return to their homes as their families had fled. A promised centre for returnees had not been built. The report went on:

> He and his companions then rented a room and went into hiding until they could escape to other countries. He told us: "I left home because throughout Afghanistan I am not safe. I and a few boys found a rented room; we were hidden in this room and day by day we escaped to neighbouring countries. The weather in Kabul and all over Afghanistan was so cold and I had nothing to wear and I could not buy. So I really spent very bad days of frigid weather. In Nauru the hottest, in Afghanistan the coldest!"
>
> Thinking that his family by then might be in Pakistan or Iran, Rajab spent a year searching for them without success. He returned to Afghanistan once and in his home town learned that members of a fundamentalist sect had seized his family's house and land. His family's story had been spread around that sect's political group, so that none of them were safe in Afghanistan. Escaping an assassination attempt, he fled into a neighbouring country where he lives in hiding, still not safe: "I live in this country illegally and any time police can catch me or they can blame me for any crime as it has happened to me before."
>
> When interviewed he had not been able to find his family and is not confident for the future: "I could not succeed to find them yet. It is impossible for me and for my family to go to my homeland and this issue can never be solved who ever comes (to power) in Afghanistan."

While the report found that Australia had sent or attempted to send asylum seekers to unsafe places, Amanda Vanstone rejected this conclusion, saying the report fell into "the realm of unsubstantiated assertion masquerading as fact."

Responding to a series of questions I emailed to the immigration department, an official said the Jangalak centre in Kabul, built to accommodate those returning to Afghanistan, had commenced operations on 1 July 2003. The department had provided $1.1 million to assist in the refurbishment and initial operations of the centre and $575,000 towards its running costs. Some 353 asylum seekers had voluntarily returned to Afghanistan before 30 June 2003. Like Rajab, they would not have had the benefit of the centre. Sixty-seven had voluntarily returned since the centre opened, 56 of them accepting the Australian government's voluntary return package. "Before the opening of the Jangalak centre, returnees were not promised or provided ongoing accommodation in Kabul. Returnees were provided overnight accommodation if they were returning to other destinations within Afghanistan," the official said.

On the question of whether the government monitored the fate of those who returned, the official's response said: "It is the government's policy not to monitor non-Australian citizens in foreign countries. Where it is assessed as part of a protection determination process that there is no real chance of persecution of the claimant on return, Australia is not responsible for the future wellbeing of people in their homeland." As for the allegations that people had been returned to unsafe or dangerous situations:

> People in any country can face dangers, disadvantages and uncertainty. This does not mean that we have obligations to them under the Refugees Convention and it does not automatically establish some entitlement to obtain residence in a country of choice. The ERC [Edmund Rice Centre] has reported a number of assertions, but has made no real attempt to test those assertions.
>
> The department may guess in some cases at the identity of persons cited as case studies, but has found nothing to substantiate

the assertions made about those persons being in danger or disadvantaged after being returned. Again, if anyone has any additional or new information about these cases, DIMIA [the immigration department] is ready to look into them.

The response was dismissed by Phil Glendenning, the director of the Edmund Rice Centre, who told me the centre had presented all its material to the department in Sydney, Canberra and Geneva on no fewer than seven occasions. "The bottom line is that the government cannot say this isn't true because they don't do this monitoring. They don't know." He added that three of the 40 in the study had since been accepted as refugees in the United Kingdom, Canada and New Zealand. "What is it that Canada, New Zealand and the UK understand about what it is to be a refugee that we clearly don't?"

Another issue was raised by David Corlett in his book, *Following Them Home*, published in mid-2005. As he put it: "Countless numbers of failed asylum seekers have been returned with psychological problems stemming largely from their experiences while under Australia's duty of care." Returnees had spoken of ongoing sleep difficulties, persistent headaches and being socially withdrawn, "not wanting to be around people since their experience in Australia's detention centres."

·

On a cool autumn day in 2004, Beth Mackenzie prepared to do something she had never done before. The 82-year-old drove the 110 kilometres from her tiny farm at Buchan to the Victorian country town of Bairnsdale to address her first public meeting. The occasion was a community forum to be chaired by the Labor leader, Mark Latham, something he called "democracy in the raw." Mackenzie patiently waited for her opportunity to take the microphone and delivered a powerful speech on the plight of one of the Nauru asylum seekers.

Latham's unorthodox leadership and aspirational politics seemed to be connecting with the electorate at the time and there was no shortage of people wanting to raise an issue, from the war in Iraq to the plight of the disabled. But it was Mackenzie who drew the loudest ovation. Picking up on one of Latham's pet themes, the need for parents to read to their children at night and his own commitment to his two small boys, she told how the woman on Nauru was in need of urgent surgery to save her sight. "She will never be able to read to her two little boys," she said. "She hasn't been given the medical attention for her eyes that was recommended two and a half years ago. Very soon she will be blind."

Latham responded that Labor would close down the Howard government's Pacific Solution, but did not seem to relate to Mackenzie's compassion. "The ignored or neglected migration issue in Australia is the 30,000 illegal migrant workers in this country taking jobs off Australians and running down Australian working conditions," he said.

Mackenzie was oblivious to the response. Having mustered the courage to speak, she was just glad to have done what she considered to be the right thing by the Iraqi woman and buoyed by the number of people who followed her out to her car to express their support for her stand. It was several months earlier at Bairnsdale that Mackenzie had been moved by a production by Rural Actors for Refugees. Then she watched a *Compass* program on ABC television dealing with the many ways Australians had devoted their time to supporting and assisting asylum seekers to cope with the demands of detention or their temporary visa status. Given her remote location in country Victoria, she decided the best thing she could do was write to someone in detention, so she made contact with the organisation that produced the play in Bairnsdale. Soon, she had two people to correspond with, both of them on Nauru.

The first letter she received back was from a woman who was on the island with her husband and two young children. (Now living in Australia on a temporary protection visa and concerned about relatives in Iraq, the woman asked not to be identified by name in this book.) Expressing her joy at having someone to "write to me in friendship," the woman concluded that first letter: "Can you imagine when your child asks you about many things, but you find yourself in a state of weakness. I have a feeling of desperation after this long time which we spent in detention. I wish to see my children in good clothes, in new clothes. I wish to buy my big child a camera because he is fond of photos. But I can't buy a camera for him. We can't achieve to our children their wishes. We are useless parents."

Mackenzie replied immediately, telling the woman she was not a useless parent and offering understanding. "I was very sad, very touched by her," she later reflected. Many letters later, in February 2004, the woman revealed that she was going blind. A specialist, Robert Nave, had examined her in December 2001 and advised those running the camp that the only treatment for her condition was bilateral corneal grafting, a procedure that could not be performed on Nauru. The operation required good-quality donor tissue, skilled surgery and prolonged follow-up, the specialist advised, adding that there was no urgency. The same specialist examined the woman almost two years later and his letter expressed measured concern that her condition had been allowed to go untreated for so long. He understood she had family connections in Australia and added: "I would be grateful if consideration could be given to expediting her case as soon as possible on both medical and humanitarian grounds."

Well before this point had been reached, Beth Mackenzie had begun devoting almost every waking hour to the woman's cause. "I lived it, day and night," she later said. "I would get up in the middle of the night to write to politicians, Labor and Liberal, and DIMIA. I really didn't know my way around. I'd never heard of DIMIA in my life. I'd vaguely heard of Woomera. It just became one of the most important things at the top of my mind because how could I resist the letters she was writing?" How could she indeed?

In April, the woman wrote that after two and a half years she was "just hearing promises without any action." She went on:

All the patients here sent to Australia for treatment except me. Why? Why? Although my problem is a difficult one, they are closing their eyes for me. They ignored my difficult problem and what's the meaning of my life without eyes? I just want to ask them: who can stay in the same place one week, not two and a half years and maybe more and more? Where's the mercy? What's our crime? What's our children's crime? Please Beth help me as soon as possible because I have depend on you completely if you can and I am very thankful that you are a kind person. I shall keep watching for your mails. God bless you.

In her desperation, Mackenzie contacted the Fred Hollows Foundation and extracted the mobile number of its chief executive, Mike Lynskey, who was in Africa. "She just came across as an ordinary citizen who was appalled by what was happening and wanted to do something," Lynskey recalled. A plan was devised for the woman to be treated at a Sydney hospital by a specialist who would waive the fee, though Mackenzie, a pensioner, was prepared to mount a fund-raising campaign. "We could see the connection, that this was somebody who did not deserve to be in that position and needed some help," Lynskey explained. "And it was not going to be a big deal to provide it. There were plenty of ophthalmologists in Australia who were willing to help." And Mackenzie? "She kept phoning and phoning, followed every step along the way and never missed a beat to make sure it all happened."

In the end, the plan was not needed. The woman was flown by the department from Nauru to undergo surgery in Adelaide. With her husband and sons, she was afforded temporary protection. I spoke to Mackenzie on the day she received the news that the woman was finally coming to Australia. She was almost deliriously happy, and told how she had danced around the kitchen and cried tears of joy.

CHAPTER 4

Truth and hope

*The offshore reassessment process was designed to obviate the need
for any professional assistance to those on Nauru.*

– Robert Illingworth, Assistant Secretary,
Onshore Protection, Department of Immigration,
Multiculturalism and Indigenous Affairs

O n 22 February 2005, I submitted a formal application for a
visa to visit Nauru. Although he was still in the Nauruan
parliament, Rene Harris was no longer president. The
reformist government of Ludwig Scotty had been given an
emphatic mandate in the election held in October 2002 to resolve a
constitutional deadlock. A visit would be an opportunity to finally
write first-hand about the people in the camps and how the new
government was coming to grips with the tiny island's impover-
ished state.

The application form allowed just two lines to explain the
nature of business to be conducted and I was suitably circumspect.
"Keen to interview senior government figures and write about
future of Nauru," I wrote. What I wanted was to put my case to
someone in the new government, but attempts to contact the relevant people on the island had come to nothing.

For weeks, my daily routine involved placing a call to the Nauru
government and asking for the relevant minister or official. Initially

Ali Alsaai with his wife Widad and their daughter Banin
Photo: Craig Abraham, courtesy of *The Age*

– and this went on for a fortnight – I was told I should speak to the chief secretary, but she was invariably indisposed. When I asked for the president, I was told to ring back tomorrow. Then I was informed that the foreign minister, David Adeang, was the appropriate person. He, too, proved elusive. By mid-March every switchboard operator on *The Age* knew the Nauru government's phone number off by heart, but I was no closer to going.

In the meantime, I learned that Houda al-Massaudi, one of the remaining Iraqis on Nauru, was in Australia with her husband for treatment and staying at the Maribyrnong Immigration Detention Centre. If I could not go to Nauru, I could at least speak to one of the Nauru detainees in Melbourne. I arranged with the refugee advocate Pamela Curr to pay them a visit. At roughly the same time, the handful of Liberal MPs who had been quietly pushing for a more just and humane approach to asylum seekers behind the scenes were running short of patience. Among them was John Forrest, the National Party member for the Victorian seat of Mallee, who argued that temporary protection visa holders – many of whom picked fruit or worked in abattoirs – did "jobs Australians don't want to do" and had become valued members of rural communities. But it was Petro Georgiou, whose Melbourne seat of Kooyong had formerly been held by Andrew Peacock and Sir Robert Menzies, who went public with his call for fundamental change early in February. As he told parliament:

> Our policies towards asylum seekers were premised on concern about vast numbers of undeserving and potentially dangerous people landing on our shores. Today, unauthorised boat arrivals have all but ceased and the great majority of people they carried have turned out to be genuine refugees. There were no terrorists hiding amongst the asylum seekers. Globally the number of refugees has nearly halved during the last decade. Of particular significance to Australia is the fact that refugees have stopped flowing from Afghanistan and Iraq, two of the main source countries of asylum seekers coming here without visas.
>
> If a crisis situation justifies severe measures and the crisis passes, on what basis can the severe measures be perpetuated? In brief, I believe that we need to release asylum seekers in detention, of whom there are only a couple of hundred, who have passed health and security checks and place them in the community until their applications have been processed. I believe that thousands of genuine refugees who have temporary protection visas should be given permanent residence in a one-off amnesty.

Of particular concern to Georgiou were those who posed no threat to the Australian community, but had been detained indefinitely. "The average prison sentence for people convicted of rape and other sexual crimes in Victoria and New South Wales is just over four years and it is between two and three years for offenders guilty of robbery, abduction or kidnapping," Georgiou said. "In Australia's immigration detention centres there are people who have been locked up for more than four years, the longest being for more than six years. These people are detained indefinitely, potentially for life, because they have been found to be ineligible for an Australian visa and we cannot find another country to accept them."

Two days after his speech to Parliament, I interviewed Georgiou at a Canberra restaurant. This was an unusual event in itself, as he has always been one of those rare politicians who are content to assume a low public profile. His best work has been as hard-headed professional, devising winning strategies for election campaigns, or as passionate defender of minorities and advocate for human rights, usually in the privacy of the party room. Extracting a juicy quote from the 57-year-old has always been a task requiring more than a little patience. But this time, when I pressed him on why he had taken a public stand, he delivered a succinct reply that explained why so many Australians had taken up the cause of those hurt by Australia's policy of border protection. "In life, do you know how many things you'd like to walk past and not notice?" he asked. "Lots. But sometimes you do notice, and when you notice, you have to do something."

The government's response was less than encouraging. On 23 March, Vanstone offered a modest concession, one that turned out to be no more than a titbit. A new visa would be created to enable those whose claims had been rejected and who had been in detention for a very long period the prospect of being allowed into the community until they could be removed. It would be called a "removal pending" bridging visa, and it had no implications for those on Nauru.

When someone asked why it was all right to detain people indefinitely on Nauru if it was now not all right to detain them indefinitely on the mainland, the minister explained that the Australian caseload was "quite different" from the cases on Nauru, and that offshore processing had been "one of the most successful weapons against people smugglers." She went on:

Now, let's make no bones about this. People pay people smugglers not to get away from adversity, because they're already away from it when they're in Indonesia. They're already away from that which they are fleeing. What they're paying a people smuggler for is to get into Australia in order to get a migration outcome.

So the quickest and the most effective way to put people smugglers out of business is to make sure that the people smugglers, as best we can, cannot land on the mainland and therefore that their very sorry cargo will end up in offshore processing centres. Now you can see that by the maintenance of offshore processing centres, people smuggling has been brought to an end."

When another reporter asked if the Nauru caseload would be looked at again, Vanstone said it had been given a "pretty good going over" the previous year, when 146 of the remaining 176 Afghans had been found to be refugees on the basis of changed circumstances in Afghanistan and 27 of the remaining Iraqis were resettled in Australia. The message was that those remaining on Nauru were the bottom of the asylum seeker barrel. They had been assessed more than once and been found not to be deserving of protection. They were the last 54 of the 1232 asylum seekers who have been accommodated on Nauru. But this was not the message from Marion Le, who had exhaustively reviewed many of the cases.

A few months earlier, the remaining 29 Afghans had written her a letter, urging her to "report our deplorable condition to the responsible department and urge them to find a proper solution for our endless suffering." The letter concluded:

We have been detained in Nauru since 2001 and we are extremely tired of being in detention, we possess the right like other human beings to be free and freedom is the natural right of every human beings. No one oppose freedom if there is justice in the world.

As you are aware that Australian government has constantly been putting pressure on us for deportation, the same pressure cause us to suffer physically and mentally. Most of us are going through various difficulties and it will affect our body to suffer till the end of our lives.

There is no possible way for us to return back and we can no longer bear being in detention. Therefore, we constantly and humbly request from you to act appropriately and fairly to terminate our endless incarceration.

The pressure to return voluntarily was a constant theme in letters from those detained on Nauru to their Australian "families." Late in November, for instance, Aslam Kazimi wrote to Dorothy Babb in Sydney after seeking to add some information to his application for protection. The immigration department official had rebuffed his request, he wrote, adding:

He brought me a message and said that Australian government vowed not to accept the remaining Afghan asylum seekers on Nauru and he asked me to let my friends know that Australia is not going to accept you and there is no alternative for you, unless you have to return back or would be under the responsible of IOM [International Organization for Migration]. It is all added to our distressed loneliness and ordeals. I began to realise that depression and sorrows are the things which closest to death, and we are all paralysed and disappointed by the constant pressures which DIMIA imposes on us.

Yesterday I respectfully asked from the DIMIA officer how do you expected from a person who grow up in the climate of war shattered country to clearly express his or her fears in the last three interviews to be recognised as refugees, then he angrily mentioned that is your fault and he added he is not the decision maker, the only thing he is going to offer us [is] returning back. Please let your friends know that we are not able to return and we are not supposed to stay in detention for ever.

Those remaining on Nauru had no way of knowing how hard Le and her assistants, Claire Bruhns and Emrys Nekvapil, had been working on their behalf since the last rejections in May 2004. Having had access to the files of all of those who had been rejected, Le was convinced that serious mistakes had been made. Moreover, she had gathered evidence backing the claims of many who had said they were from Afghanistan but had been rejected on the basis that their nationality was in doubt. Finally, there was new information that the security situation in some parts of Afghanistan had worsened, convincing Le that that many of the rejected cases now had a stronger case than they had in mid-2004. In a letter sent to Vanstone on 24 March, Le asked that all the remaining Aghan, Iraqi and Iranian cases on Nauru be re-opened on the basis of new information. As Le later explained: "There were some very, very odd decisions made on the ones who are left there."

A few days after her letter to Vanstone, Le received a letter from Robert Illingworth, an immigration official responsible for onshore processes. He assured her that information passed by her to the department had been considered before those remaining had been rejected and that they all had the opportunity to have a representative with them or submit material on their behalf. The letter included one statement that was, at best, puzzling. "The offshore reassessment process was designed to obviate the need for any professional assistance to those on Nauru."

Le replied the same day, 29 March, pointing out that in the majority of cases the new information submitted had not been placed on the case files. She also explained that she had not been present at any of the re-examination interviews with the Afghans because of delays in processing her visa application. "Suffice to say, the Aghan applicants had no power over whether or not I was able to be present at their re-examination interviews." As for the statement about the offshore process "obviating" the need for any professional assistance, Le said it needed to be examined. The *Pocket Oxford Dictionary* defined obviate as "to meet and get rid of, or prevent (difficulties, objections, etc) by effective measures." Far from being in need of "obviation," Le said her role in representing the Nauru asylum seekers had been acknowledged in a media release from no lesser source than Amanda Vanstone.

•

Houda al-Massaudi shuffled into the reception area with the aid of a walking frame, her thin body bent with pain. She gave a shy, nervous smile when we were introduced, but became distinctly anxious when I opened my notebook. It was mid-March 2005 during visiting hours at the Maribyrnong Immigration Detention Centre, where Houda was a temporary resident, transported from Nauru to Australia to receive medical treatment for an injured back for the second time in less than six months.

Houda was wary of strangers, especially journalists. She feared any publicity could diminish the chances of her husband Khairy and herself finally being accepted for refugee status. And who could blame her? Having survived the event that became the "children overboard" affair in October 2001 – when the Howard government asserted, wrongly, that asylum seekers had thrown their children overboard – and spent eleven days on Christmas Island, eleven months on Manus Island and more than two years on Nauru, she had become accustomed to pain and disappointment.

With Khairy, she was one of the last two Iraqi couples left on Nauru as the processing centre approached its fourth year of operation, their claims of refugee status having been rejected. The pair were among the group of 54 asylum seekers on Nauru – 29 Afghans, twenty Iraqis, two Bangladeshis, two Iranians and a Pakistani.

Houda was the first woman plucked from the sea during the children overboard episode in 2001. A belt attached to a rope was placed around her chest and she was hauled aboard HMAS *Adelaide* by the sailors. She injured her back when she landed hard on the deck of the boat. The technique was used unsuccessfully with two more women before it was decided to use another means of getting the women and children on board.

Pictures of a healthy Houda in transit in Malaysia before the episode suggest that the pain she has suffered for more than three and a half years resulted from the way in which she was rescued and inadequacy of her treatment on Nauru. In June 2003, she fell in a bathroom and fractured her pelvis, but the fracture was not detected for twelve months. On Nauru, Houda took tablets for the pain and spent all her time sitting in their hut, leaving only when Khairy carried her to the bathroom.

Pamela Curr from the Asylum Seeker Resource Centre in West Melbourne remains incensed that those on board the boat were forced to wait until it was sinking and had to enter the water before they were rescued. As she puts it: "There were children in the water all right, but it was Howard and not the parents who put them there."

On the afternoon we met, Houda displayed no bitterness toward those who rescued her. Quite the contrary. Khairy described how one sailor extricated her foot after it became stuck between two planks as the boat broke up, probably saving her life. But by the time I spoke to her she was at breaking point, like so many of the others. While the new Nauruan government had improved conditions for detainees, allowing them freedom of movement around the tiny island during daylight hours on weekdays, Khairy said he would like Australians to be able to see them and how "the life is going from them."

"They only eat, sleep, walk and sit, not seeing anything of life," he said. "They are tired, very tired." Tired, it became clear, was a euphemism for a multitude of ailments, most of them psychological.

Marion Le has worked in refugee resettlement for more than 25 years and is not prone to displays of emotion, but Khairy said Marion cried when she saw the condition of his wife when they met on Nauru in January. The doctor who treated her in Melbourne, Rob Weller, subsequently warned that her condition would deteriorate if she was sent back to Nauru. He added that she would not recover until ongoing psychological issues, including post-traumatic stress disorder, depression, isolation and her lack of refugee status, were resolved.

Khairy, 50, and Houda, 38, fled Iraq in 1991 after Houda was so badly assaulted by Saddam's police that she lost the baby she was carrying in her womb. The couple spent the next decade in Iran, and for much of that time the former teacher eked out a living as a street vendor, reluctant to write to loved ones in Iraq for fear that they would be victimised. He does not know whether the brother and nephew they left behind are dead or alive.

Khairy said he still dreamed of having a child and declared he would work in any job, "in supermarket, anything," if he were allowed to come to Australia. "I need freedom," he said. As I left them, I promised to call by again – after I had visited the others on Nauru, I hoped. As his wife shuffled away, I noticed that only one foot touched the floor. It was then that Khairy delivered an impassioned plea: "This I need from Australia: help me. Help my wife."

Weeks later, I again visited Houda and Khairy at Maribyrnong and was struck by her improvement. They had been able to glimpse life in Melbourne through a car window as they were driven between the detention centre and the hospital, and liked what they saw. It was just so peaceful, Khairy remarked. We spoke of their hopes of living in the community and Houda said she would cook a meal for us when this day came. Within a day or so, Pamela Curr rang to express concern that, now she had been discharged from hospital, Houda was going backwards and retreating inside herself.

•

John Howard's immediate reaction to the reports that children had been thrown overboard was to declare that he did not want "people like that" in Australia and that "genuine refugees don't do that." There was no apology when it was confirmed after the election that no children were thrown overboard by those on the boat known as SIEV IV. Several of those aboard the boat were subsequently found to be refugees and resettled in Australia.

Ali Alsaai, his wife Widad and two daughters Hawraa and Banin are among this group. When I met them they were making a new life in the Melbourne suburb of Footscray. The family had spent several months in offshore detention on Manus Island and a year at the Maribyrnong Immigration Detention Centre after Hawraa was diagnosed with diabetes. Ali told me the thing that hurt him and other parents most about the children overboard allegation was the implication that they were bad parents. "We come from a society where we are family-oriented. We are very close to family members. We don't throw our children overboard." To emphasise the point, he said that if he was offered the world in return for his daughter's finger, "I wouldn't upset it."

While the family was at Maribyrnong, Hawraa, then aged 16, was enrolled at Footscray City College. Peter Noss, a year 8 coordinator, was assigned the task of making her transition as smooth as possible. One of his first acts was to organise a "whip around" of the staff to help set the family up in their modest unit. "I was struck immediately by how bright and intelligent she was," Noss recalled. "I just felt so sorry for their predicament. I didn't know anything about detention centres and I'd like to think I'd be the same with any kid who needed a bit of a bunk up."

Towards the end of the first year, Noss recalled waiting outside the school with Hawraa, who was to go to the Royal Childrens Hospital for a check-up. "We're waiting for the car to pick her up and she says, 'Here they come!' It's a van from the detention centre with a light on the top, blacked out windows and bars, and I thought, 'What's going on?' There were two people in the front of the van. One's got out, undone the big padlock on the side of the door and slid the door back and here is the rest of the family, sitting inside this darkened van. We shake hands. 'Hello.' 'Hello.' 'See you soon.' Hawraa gets in. 'Bye.' Close the door and a huge big padlock is put on the door. Well, that did it for me. I just broke up."

The other episode that mystified Noss was when Hawraa came to school one day and explained that she was returning to Papua New Guinea because, under the Pacific Solution, boat people seeking refugee status had to be processed offshore. "So they've sent the family, a nurse, a guard and God knows what else, gone up there, stayed in a hotel, which was fantastic for the family, and the next day they've said: 'We've granted you a temporary protection visa. You can go anywhere in Australia.' Hawraa said, 'I want to go back to Footscray because my friends are at school there'. That's why they're back at Footscray."

Now in year 11, Hawraa continued to excel at school, according to Noss, and was more than capable of realising her ambition to become a doctor. Banin, affectionately called "Banana" by her classmates, wanted to be a teacher. Hawraa was a shy girl who had neither concealed her situation from her classmates and teachers, nor advertised it. She wanted to be treated like everybody else. When I wrote an article about the family for *The Age* she didn't want her picture to appear. A few weeks earlier, her creative writing teacher, Emma Pollock, asked the class to write two short pieces, one on the things that made them happy, the other on the things that made them angry.

Hawraa's first piece began: "I'm really happy because I left detention centre and I hope everyone will. I'm really happy because I came to this school and have very nice teachers and friends." The second piece concluded: "It's really hard for people who left their country to be in a safe place but they are kept in detention centres. I have been in a detention centre before and I understand how these people feel." This girl, who had crossed the ocean in a boat that sank, called her piece "Refugees like this fish want their freedom." Pollock says that, for the first time in her career, she was moved to tears by the work of a student.

With limited access to English training because of their temporary status, Hawraa's parents were making slower progress. Both hoped to gain permanent protection, get jobs and be joined by their three sons (one of whom now has two sons of his own). Since they left Iraq, their home in Najaf had been destroyed in a bomb blast. A month earlier, Alsaai's cousin died when he was hit by stray fire from a helicopter gunship, leaving behind a pregnant wife. Hawraa said it was hard being separated from her brothers, who regularly spoke by phone to their mother.

Ali Alsaai walked for hours at a time each day, tinkered with the car he hoped one day to drive, and worried about his sons. When I asked Widad what she liked most about Australia, she smiled broadly. "The people. Very nice," she said, gently pounding her fist on her heart.

•

Towards the end of March I had a minor breakthrough in my efforts to visit Nauru. I finally had the chance to speak to David Adeang. It seemed that my request for a visa had gone astray, so he asked me to fax it again. He also asked to see some recent pieces I had written for *The Age*. I faxed the application and the articles, but there was no quick response.

Concerned that it might still come to nothing, I proceeded with a feature article about those who remained on Nauru, based on my contact with the Massaudis, emails from a number of asylum seekers and interviews with Le, their pro bono migration agent, and some of their supporters in Australia.

Abuozar al-Salem was among the young Iraqi men still on the island. He was a teenager when his boat was intercepted and he was taken first to Christmas Island, then to Manus, and finally to Nauru. His brother Fares fled Saddam Hussein's Iraq much earlier, after the first Gulf War. After spending four years in a refugee camp in Saudi Arabia, Fares was accepted by Australia as a refugee. He lives with his wife and four children in country Victoria.

When I contacted him, Fares did not know the circumstances of his younger brother's departure from Iraq, but he had no doubt he left in fear for his life. Nor did he know whether his father, who was treated brutally by Saddam's regime, or another brother were still alive. Fares had written to immigration authorities offering to take responsibility for his brother but the offer was rejected.

Le was especially worried about the emotional state of Abuozar and another young Iraqi whose mother had been murdered after he fled his homeland. The second young man also had family in Australia, but Le said his story of his mother's murder was not believed by those who assessed his claim for refugee status on Nauru. "Family members here could have verified at least part of the story and there was a death certificate provided which said very clearly that she had been shot four times," Le said. "That boy, when I interviewed him, was really highly disturbed, as anyone would be."

There were just two families with children still in the camp, both claiming to be from Afghanistan. Le told me that it was now clear that one of the families, the Hussainis, who had been rejected on the basis that they were Pakistanis, were from Afghanistan, as they maintained from the outset. "When all the reassessments were being done," she said, "the father was lining up to get his decision like everybody else and he said it never for one minute occurred to him that the assessment process wouldn't be successful. He'd gone in, told his story, didn't lie. When he came back out, his little girl, Zahra, said, 'Daddy, Daddy, did we get the visa?' Not wanting to disappoint her, he answered: 'Yes, yes, we got the visa.' And she replied: 'If you got the visa, why are you crying?' He later told me he never thought he would have to lie to his own daughter."

The departmental file on the Hussaini family provided a clue to the culture of scepticism that has confronted the Nauru asylum seekers from the outset. In each family member's file is their name, age and the number of their boat. When it came to the youngest child, Saqlain Abbas, who was born on 14 September 2002, the file says: "Claims to have been born on Nauru." Where else could he have been born on that date?

The feature article also introduced readers to Ali Mullaie, who had arrived on Nauru as a teenager and was now 22. This young man's name had kept coming up when I spoke with those who had been accepted as refugees and resettled in Australia and New Zealand after spending lengthy periods on Nauru. Many credited him with teaching them English and preparing them for the challenges that lay ahead. Among them was Mahmood Baqir, a year 9 student in Canberra. "He was just unbelievable. He did everything for everyone," Mahmood told me. "He serves the Nauruan students and the Nauruan people without any payment. One of the ambitions of my life is to see him once again."

The Tarren-Sweeney family in Newcastle were one of dozens of Australian households who wrote to the Nauru asylum seekers offering support and sending phone cards so they could maintain contact with the outside world. Mullaie interpreted the letters exchanged by Savannah Tarren-Sweeney and the young Afghan girls. Over time, she came to consider Mullaie as part of her family. "He is an inspirational person. He never thinks badly of anybody and he tries really hard to improve everybody else's lot," said Savannah's mother, Georgina, who sent Mullaie a second-hand laptop to help with his teaching. So appreciative were the locals that a group of Nauruan teachers arrived at the camp to celebrate his twenty-first birthday, she said.

When he was not teaching, Mullaie wrote poems about loneliness and grief and the emptiness of being imprisoned. One included this verse:

Warm gale...!
As warm as a mother's heart.
Caresses the sun-burned skin on my face.
I contemplate blue sky,
But crouch by the wall of a swallow's cage.

Le believed there were two main reasons genuine refugees had been consistently rejected on Nauru: a failure by bureaucrats to verify their accounts, particularly with family members who had been accepted as refugees and were living in Australia, and the mistaken belief on the part of some asylum seekers that, if they told the truth, they would be refused. Some, for instance, were told by people smugglers not to mention that they had large families because this information was likely to prejudice their chances. Others, like the Massaudis, did not initially mention the assault that caused Houda to miscarry because she was too embarrassed to show the scars.

"We believe that all of the Afghans should be immediately brought to Australia," Le told me. "Of the Iraqis, there is no one there who hasn't got a reason for leaving Iraq when they left and, at this point, the United Nations is still saying they can't go back. At the moment anyone who has had anything to do with Westerners is being targeted. If they turn up back there, they run the risk of their whole families being wiped out in some cases."

The story was published on 28 March 2005 under the headline "The Forgotten," along with pictures sent by the asylum seekers to their Australian supporters. Two days later, I received an email from Ali Mullaie, who was pleased I had made contact and told how he had recently broken his arm when he fell off his bike:

> Recently I have been very susceptible to pain and intense of tensions on my mind, I often concentrate too much but not clearly focus on doing things properly and mostly confused. But lately I fall down on the street during I was cycling because I was thinking on that moment and did not know where I was.
>
> I was thinking about my unending journey and about my uncertainty situation, I thought I'm engulfing in darkness and in seeking someone to rescue me from this darkness but suddenly I was fallen on the ground with huge pain on my left hand by then I found that it was broken.

A few days later I wrote an email to David Adeang, expressing frustration that I had been unable to reach him by telephone. I told him I was still keen to write a story on the country's future and, quite separately, "I would also like to do a piece on the young fellow from the migration processing camp who is teaching in the Nauru school." I stressed that I would need to visit that month, before federal parliament resumed for the budget session. I received Adeang's reply at 6.35 the following morning, Tuesday 5 April. It read:

> Michael,
>
> I have instructed the department of Foreign Affairs to process your visa; kindly contact our Consulate-General in Melbourne; I have indicated that you are welcome to visit at any time to your convenience. I have no travel plans until end of the month.
>
> Look forward to seeing you here.
>
> Rgds, David

The next flight to Nauru would leave Brisbane at 2 o'clock on Thursday morning. Within a matter of hours, I had secured a copy of my visa from the consulate in Melbourne and booked my ticket.

The Rehmati family
Photo: Michael Gordon, courtesy of *The Age*

CHAPTER 5

Six days on Nauru

When we had the resources, there was absolutely no political will for good governance. Now, when we have the will, we have no resources.

— David Adeang, finance minister, Nauru government

The detention camp is a small jail and the island is a big jail. All of the island, same jail. I want to get freedom.

— Monawir al-Saber

With less than 24 hours to prepare for the trip, I was unable to book accommodation at either of the two Nauru hotels. The main one, the Menen, was booked out (apart from the very expensive presidential suite) and the phones had been down at the Oden Aiwo. But I did discover a few things about staying on the island. There were no taxis or hire car companies and no businesses accepted credit cards or cheques. The world's smallest independent republic was strictly a cash economy. The Air Nauru flight from Brisbane stopped over at Honiara and arrived just before 10 am, when the Nauruan parliament was scheduled to meet.

There were plenty of spare seats in the big plane, but it was not the most relaxed of journeys. Aside from wondering if the decision to give me a visa would be reversed on my arrival, as it had for others, there were plenty of other uncertainties, including whether

I would be allowed inside the processing camp. The first hurdle was cleared when immigration officials accepted the visa and took possession of my passport, saying I could retrieve it in a day or two. With no transport organised, I was lucky that the officer in charge of the Australian High Commission on Nauru, Colin Milner, was picking up his assistant. He gave me a lift to the very downmarket Oden Aiwo hotel, which had plenty of rooms and was quite close to the parliament. It was clear that the arrival of a journalist was the source of some sensitivity, if not consternation. I tried to make small talk by asking how the new government was travelling. Milner said he would need a clearance to talk to me before he could offer an answer. But he did drop me off at parliament after I checked into the hotel.

Nauru time, like Fiji time, tends to be elastic. There was no sign of activity in parliament when I arrived, though it was well after 10 o'clock. I found David Adeang, whose portfolios included finance, internal affairs and foreign affairs, in the ministerial reception area. He was warm and friendly, introducing me to several of his ministerial colleagues and agreeing to give me a tour of the island the next day, a public holiday. Then it was time for parliament and he directed me to the public gallery.

With no newspapers and limited news coverage on television or radio, the gallery was packed with families and individuals, many of them keen to know what was going to happen to their pay, others probably keen to escape the heat and humidity outside. The scene inside the air-conditioned parliament had an almost surreal quality. The politicians all wore pressed white shirts and ties and followed the Westminster tradition under watchful eye of the Speaker, Valdon K. Dowiyogo, beginning with matters of privilege, condolence motions, ministerial statements and questions without notice.

One of the first items of business was a condolence motion for Pope John Paul II, who had passed away the previous week. The members were invited to stand for two minutes as a mark of respect and all but one responded. Ever the recalcitrant, isolated and without influence, Rene Harris remained in his seat.

After getting a feel of how things worked, my priority was to get a vehicle. At a nearby shop, a young woman offered to drive me to a house where I could hire a car. She had recently given up her university studies in Fiji and seemed resigned to a future without prosperity but with her family. Everything on Nauru was falling down, she said. She had time to kill and became interested when I told her I was a journalist and that I was keen to visit the asylum seekers' camp. We circumnavigated the island, visited the now empty, but still maintained, Topside Camp and paused at State House, where the last 54 asylum seekers were living. I introduced myself to Shamel Mahmoodi, who ran the facility on behalf of the International Organisation for Migration, and he politely informed me that I would need a letter of authority from the Nauru government if I wanted to enter the camp. By the time my guide dropped me at my car, I had a good sense of where things were, particularly the turn-off from the main road that led to the camp.

That afternoon I called by the Civic Centre, where a weeklong workshop was attempting to instil in the island's school teachers a new approach to education, one that placed a high premium on building self-reliance. Despite the reality of crumbling infrastructure and insufficient funds, the mood was positive. One of the workshop moderators, Paul Sutton, was a Queensland public servant with wide experience working with indigenous communities on Cape York. "I have never seen a group of people collectively with such a positive view of life, despite everything around them," he said of the Nauruans. "They are determined to somehow get up, but they don't yet know how to do it. What they have are clues."

Unlike indigenous communities struggling to shake the legacy of decades of passive welfare, Nauruans had been required to make a very rapid adjustment from a situation in which their natural wealth from their phosphate reserves meant they could buy whatever help they needed. "Now they can't buy help and they've got to figure how to do things for themselves – and that involves a serious change in mindset," Sutton said. "It's a bit like asking Prince Charles to wash the dog. He wouldn't have a clue!"

I didn't realise it at the time, but while I was at the workshop several of the Afghan asylum seekers were in the internet cafe below. Ali Mullaie was among them. He had seen me arrive and suspected I might the journalist who had sent him an email foreshadowing a visit. Although he was now a full-time voluntary teacher at Nauru College, someone at the school forgot to write a letter to the camp requesting his presence at the workshop. Not for the first time, he felt excluded.

•

The next morning, Colin Milner called by my hotel, having been cleared to give me a briefing on what Australia was doing in Nauru. After we shared breakfast and chatted about Australia's aid program, I met Adeang at his office. The power was off, as it is for several hours every day, so he gave me a handwritten note authorising my visit to the asylum seeker camp. Then we set out on a tour of the island.

One of the first stops was the president's official residence, called Cliff Lodge, where it was easy to imagine the splendour and opulence that once was Nauru. The large house and pool sit high above the area where Nauru-flagged ships were once loaded with the phosphate that made Nauruans, on a per-capita basis, second only to the Saudis as the world's richest people. "Nice view, isn't it?" asked the gently spoken Adeang. Indeed, it was. Except that the pool was empty and cracked, and the residence behind us was a burnt-out ruin.

Months after it played host to Pacific leaders and ministers, including former Australian defence minister Peter Reith, in 2001, the sprawling complex was destroyed. It is an open secret that the blaze was a protest against the profligacy, incompetence, gullibility and corruption of those who squandered Nauru's inheritance.

Adeang, 35, is the third generation of his family to be educated in Geelong, an hour south-west of Melbourne. He knows it is unrealistic to imagine recapturing anything like the level of affluence of his youth, but he does see a future for his four young children, and for Nauru. "When I was at primary school, you could look out the window at the airport and we had something like seven planes running at the time," he said. "You'd look at the ocean and we had three or four ships flying the Nauruan flag. Now we own no ships. We have one plane, but we don't even own it outright, and we can't pay the lease payments. Any time, it could be repossessed."

"When did the rot start?" I asked.

"That's what we're trying to establish," said Adeang. "We know particular administrations were known for being extremely extravagant. We know people who were particularly extravagant as well, like Rene Harris."

Even the question of what happened to the money was highly problematic, given the lack of a paper trail and the absence of government accounts for the past decade. "These former governments had a habit of, whenever they were removed from office, taking all their records with them," said Adeang. Although there were three parliamentary inquiries looking into past practices, each was limited not only by a lack of evidence but by a lack of resources. Australia was providing two senior police, as well as treasury and finance officials and an education director, but there was only one lawyer in the Nauru justice department and he was flat out investigating petty theft. "When we had the resources, there was absolutely no political will for good governance," Adeang explained. "Now, when we have the will, we have no resources."

As well as trying to explain what went wrong, the new government was working on a plan to give the country a sustainable future, with much riding on the young shoulders of Adeang and the other young ministers in Ludwig Scotty's administration, including the health minister, Kieren Keke, and the education minister, Baron Waqa. The immediate priorities involved establishing how much of the country's wealth still existed and what scope there was for secondary mining of Nauru's dwindling reserves of phosphate. The country's once massive investment portfolio, including Nauru House in Melbourne (which sold for A$140 million in November 2004) and assorted properties around the globe, had been sold to pay off debts such as the A$230 million owed to a US firm, GE Finance Corporation, but Adeang was confident there would be something left once the ledger was squared. A responsible budget had been brought down and there was confidence that Nauru would soon be removed from an international blacklist of countries tainted by money laundering.

By year's end, the new government hoped to present a plan outlining how its vision of a sustainable Nauru could be realised, but the job was being made almost impossible by the problems that confronted ministers every day – power failures, fuel shortages, bills that could not be paid, and a crumbling infrastructure, especially in the school, power generation and health systems.

Determined to share the pain and lead by example, Scotty and his ministers received a wage of $140 a fortnight, the same pay as all other public servants. But Adeang feared the amount would have to be scaled back because of a lack of money. Such a move, he conceded, would send a bad signal to the voters who endorsed pro-reform candidates for sixteen of the eighteen parliamentary seats in October 2004. "People might start thinking, 'Why bother? Maybe we made the wrong choice at the last election.'"

Three months later, as I was finishing this account, I received an email from Adeang expressing frustration that the agreement to provide refugee processing camps as part of the Pacific Solution had failed so far to deliver any real benefits to Nauru. His most recent letter from Australia's foreign minister, Alexander Downer, reported that some $70 million had been spent since 2001, but much of this went to the Australian companies providing services to the camps. "Can you believe, for instance, that it costs about $2.7 million to fund the deployment of three persons to Nauru to work in our Treasury for a year?" he asked. "This is what I was told in March."

Indeed, establishing precisely how much has been spent on the Pacific Solution, and how it was spent, is not easy. When I asked the department for a figure on the monthly cost of maintaining the Nauru camps, I was told this was not possible. "Since its introduction in September 2001, the total operational cost of the Pacific strategy (for Nauru and Manus Island only) is estimated at $207 million to 31 December 2004," the department replied, adding that this figure included set-up costs and refurbishment costs for both the Nauru and Manus centres. The 2005–06 budget papers indicated $39.5 million was spent on "the offshore management of asylum seekers" in 2004–05. The estimate for 2005–06 was almost $60 million, though it seemed likely that the actual figure would be well below this.

The biggest problem with Australia's engagement with Nauru, as far as Adeang was concerned, was that it had been solely concerned with running the processing camps, not the longer-term future of Nauru. "My view is that much of the $70 million was wasted on the corrupt government of Rene Harris, with little if any controls on how the aid should have been used," he continued. "It was simply a case of spend whatever you need to, just make sure those OPCs [off-shore processing centres] are functional and can cater for the hundreds (at one time, 1500) of refugees. So money was spent propping up a corrupt and inept government that should have been allowed to die a natural death in the interest of the longer term and sustainable future of Nauru."

His conclusion was that if Australia decided to close the camps and told Nauru its assistance was appreciated but no longer required, "Nauru would be today no better than when Australia re-discovered Nauru in 2001." Power was still unreliable despite commanding three-quarters of the Australian aid money, only one classroom had been built and the port facilities could break down any moment. Adeang's hope was that the next agreement would set out a frame-work for a relationship that was not based on maintaining the processing centres, but "securing a sustainable future for our people".

For now, however, the mood on the island was one of cautious optimism, with ordinary Nauruans generally expressing the conviction that, at the very least, they had an honest government with its feet on the ground and a genuine commitment to look to the future.

•

That afternoon, I returned to the State House camp with my note from Adeang. Over a cup of green tea, Shamel Mahmoodi explained how the restrictions had gradually been loosened since the two camps opened late in 2001. The first relaxation came early in 2002 and involved asylum seekers being allowed to leave the camp with escorts to go to the shops or the internet cafe. In September 2004, they were able to go to the shops, the internet cafe or the swimming spot where they would be observed by "zone escorts." Then, in March 2005, Adeang decided they were free to leave the camp during daylight hours on weekdays.

The physical conditions were harsh, but it seemed clear that IOM did its best to minimise the hardship of those in its care. This much was suggested by the terminology of the camp, explained to me by Mahmoodi. It was an "offshore processing centre," not a detention centre (though virtually no processing had been going on for a year); the residents were "migrants," not illegal immigrants; the security people were for the "safety" of the migrants and the "security" of the assets.

While Mahmoodi and several of the staff (and DIMIA officials) I met displayed sensitivity towards the asylum seekers, I discovered much later that discipline could be enforced with severity, depending on the whim of the Australian Federal Police Protective Services staff. For minor misdemeanours, such as being a couple of minutes late for the bus because the internet system was slow, asylum seekers could spend 24 hours, stripped naked, in the jail near the Nauru police station, where the mosquitoes were particularly bad. As one wrote: "Where ever and when ever we wish to move, we must approve from our owner for it. For single step they fixed time for us. If we miss we will treat like huge criminal and naked. We put in the jail where there is much mosquito."

I did not know of this punishment until weeks later. When I asked Ali Mullaie about it, he explained that the hostility displayed by a minority of the staff dissipated over the years, as they came to realise that the asylum seekers were not bad people. This raised a broader question: to what extent was the abuse of asylum seekers in detention the product of the negative stereotype propagated by the Howard government and encapsulated in the prime minister's words during the children overboard saga. "I don't want people like that in Australia," he had said. As the old saying goes: the fish rots from the head down.

When I wrote to Mahmoodi and asked about this form of punishment, he replied by email:

> The migrants are on special purpose visa in Nauru and their visa has several conditions. One of the conditions under the current freedom of movement is that they have to return to the camp by 7 pm. If they do not return to the camp by the 7 pm they are breaching their visa conditions, police are notified and most of the time they will counsel the migrant, if the action is repeated, they will take the migrant into custody and the police will keep the migrants for 24 hours and charge him for breaching visa condition. Since the open camp start in March 2005 we do not have any incident that police took some to custody for breaching the visa. [In] most of the cases they are counselled.

When Mahmoodi referred to "police," he was referring to both the Nauru Police Force and Australian Protective Services.

The camp sits behind a high wire fence, with a boom gate and sentry box at the entrance. There is no razor wire. On one side is a line of buildings including a modest library and a computer room. On the other side is the accommodation. In between is an open area where a volleyball court can be set up. No one was in sight; the asylum seekers were either away from the complex or in their rooms. Mahmoodi made it plain that he was happy for me to return and interview those who wanted to speak to me, but I should confine my visit to one day. With my return flight on Tuesday and the camp closed for the weekend, Monday would be the day.

A short drive from the camp is the best swimming spot on Nauru, a small boat harbour that is more like a very large ocean pool. After leaving the camp I went for a swim and met a few of the Afghans. I had hopes of finding Ali Mullaie but on the way back to the hotel I noticed the temperature gauge in my car was extremely high. I made it back to the shop where I had arranged the hire and dropped it off. Then, as I was being dropped back at my hotel, I noticed Shamel Mahmoodi in his IOM car. I flagged him down and he said he had an idea where I might find Ali. It was now mid-afternoon and we drove to the Chinese shopping precinct near Nauru College.

Mullaie was sitting, chatting to a store keeper, when I approached. He was wearing a white tee-shirt and his left arm was in plaster, the result of the bicycle accident. He was warm and friendly, and explained that he was hoping the principal of the college would drop by so that he could enter his classroom and make sure the computers were ready for when school resumed after a holiday on the following Tuesday.

We walked to the school and, as we waited for the principal, Mullaie told me the main threads of his story. He described how he had been forced to flee his home in the district of Jaghoori in Afghanistan in 2001, leaving behind his parents and six younger siblings. After his father was arrested twice by the Taliban, the family's home had been searched for weapons and his life had been threatened because he was an "infidel." It was then that his family decided he should flee. "They just wanted to get me out of there," he said. The arrangements with a people smuggler were made by his sister's husband and he had no idea that his intended destination was Australia until he reached Indonesia. There was no time to take family pictures or for proper goodbyes. Mullaie told me that he now struggled to visualise his younger siblings.

He also spoke of the pain of having his application for refugee status repeatedly rejected, and bidding farewell to friends whose applications had been accepted. "For 24 hours, or two days, or three days [after the others left], my heart has been burning, feeling it's the end of my life," he said. "But unfortunately, it is not one time, two times, three times. Many times it has happened, especially the last time."

The last time was the hardest because Mullaie was absolutely convinced he would be accepted. So, too, it seemed, was just about everybody else inside the camp. It was 15 May 2004 when 44 Afghans received their decisions. Forty were accepted and Mullaie was one of four rejected. "I really could feel like all my body been numb," he recalled. One of the IOM staff sensed his distress and offered to help him leave the area. "I said, 'No, I can walk.' But I tried to walk and it was very hard."

Mahmoodi, himself an Afghan refugee, later recalled how he was told of the decision by radio and came immediately to offer support. "It's not the end of the world," he told Ali. "You're still young, with your whole future ahead of you. Maybe this is God's will." Mullaie asked to be taken to the internet cafe and conveyed the news to Le, who had visited the camp weeks earlier to help asylum seekers prepare their applications. "You may recognise me," his email began. "I told you my story why I am not being able to return back to my country. You hugged me and cried with me when you heard my story. It is with regret to inform you that today... I received a negative decision."

We talked for perhaps an hour at Nauru College. When it became clear that the principal would not be coming, we decided to walk back towards the camp. A bus made the 30-kilometre trip around the island at regular intervals, picking up those at the shops, the internet cafe and the harbour, and Mullaie was confident that I, too, could get a lift. As we walked, children would call out to Ali from nearby houses. Some came up to say hello. One was named Dunstall, after the great Hawthorn full forward, reflecting Nauru's strong attachment to Australian Rules football. Mullaie pointed out the landmarks, including the modest house where President Scotty lived with his large extended family. Eventually, the bus came and the driver was happy enough to give me a ride.

It was almost seven o'clock when we arrived at the camp and many of those who were not on the bus were walking up the hill to meet the deadline. Among them were Ali Hussaini, his wife and two young children, as well as several other families. We agreed to see each other again on the Monday, when I would spend the day at the camp.

•

By Sunday night I had managed to hire another car from one of the staff at the hotel and explored much of the island, including the rusting cantilever that was once used to load the phosphate onto Nauru-flagged ships. A sign conveyed a warning that was just as apt for the Nauruan economy, and maybe the country too: "Danger. This structure will fall down any time." Most nights I ate alone in the dining room of the Oden Aiwo, where the menu seemed to become more limited each night and there was only ever one other guest.

One morning at one of the shops I came across one of Nauru's parliamentarians buying soft-serve ice creams for himself, his wife and their two children. It was the only luxury they could afford, he said. I also interviewed Baron Waqa, the education minister, who had one daughter working in the camp and another being taught by Ali Mullaie at Nauru College. It would hurt Nauru's economy if the camp shut down, he said, but he was sure they could manage. "We'd really like to see those people handled well and processed quickly. Some of those people have been here more than three years," he said. "It would be good to see that they get something in the end, maybe not Australia, probably another country or something. I just hope that somebody can come to their rescue. Some people up there are really suffering."

The next day would be the most important of the trip, and one of the more significant in more than three years of writing about the Pacific Solution for *The Age*. I would be the first media person given unfettered access to the camp and its population of asylum seekers. The most difficult moments would come when young men would tell me their stories of unmitigated sadness and even horror and ask what I thought. All I could offer was empathy and a link to a wider audience. One of the more awkward moments came when Mohammed Zahir Dulat Shahi asked, ever so politely: "Mr Michael,

I am wondering why you come now?" It was hard to explain how, for almost the entire time he had been endeavouring to leave Nauru, I had been seeking permission to arrive?

•

Shamel Mahmoodi had arranged for a room to be set aside for me to interview residents at the camp, but initially I chose to meet them in their rooms. Ali Mullaie assigned himself the task of making my job as easy as possible. He introduced me to those I had not met, interpreted some of the interviews and made me cups of tea.

Our first stop was the Hussaini family, one of two families that were rejected twelve months earlier when twenty families were accepted. Ali Hussaini is a big man with a generous smile. He and his wife, Batool, had kept themselves busy with embroidery during their time on the island, but he was desperately worried about how his two small children, Zahra and Saqlain, were coping with conditions there. In his first interview, the case officer accepted that the family were citizens of Afghanistan and that Hussaini's fear of the Taliban was consistent and plausible. But given that the Taliban had fallen, the claim for refugee status was rejected. While it was true that many parts of Afghanistan were insecure, the official maintained that the lawlessness applied generally rather than against any ethnic minority, such as the Hazaras.

When the Afghan caseload was reviewed in mid-2004 in the light of new information on the level of danger, the Hussaini family was rejected again, but this time on the basis that the case officer was not satisfied they were from Afghanistan. "I give my interview in English," Ali Hussaini explained to me. "I'm talking and he [the case officer] says I am from Pakistan because I am talking like an Australian. If I am Pakistani, *you* are a Pakistani."

The explanation for his accent was simple. "I learned English here," he said. "I worked in kitchen near about two years and they give me certificate. I always asked from the cooks, what you call this? I also learned from Zakir Hussain Jaffari. He already gone to New Zealand. He always told me: you should try to talk like Australians.

Now my daughter also talk like you. When we came here she was three and a half years. Now she is [seven and] talking like you. She is also Pakistani? I give my interview in English and I hope my DIMIA officer who is taking interview is very pleased about me that he is learning here, that he isn't wasting his time. I think he is very pleased for me, but look. I am rejected."

Next, I visited the extended Rehmati family, which included four children. Hussan Ali, a nephew, served as interpreter and spokesman for the group. "We heard that there this one country, Australia," he began, "who is accepting people who are refugees and they give shelter to them, so we decided to go Australia and after very danger-ous and very difficult and long journey we reached Australia and now we trapped in Nauru, so we just request to help us and take us out from here and give us shelter in your country that we can live a peaceful life, because it is very hard for us and we cannot go back to Afghanistan. We accept that we came here illegal way, but request to John Howard government... please accept us and give us shelter. It was not our fault that we came here illegal way."

He explained how one of the children, nine-year-old Abbas Ali, was ill for ten days after their last rejection. "When his father took him to the doctor, he said, 'Your son is very lonely. There is no treat-ment.'" His older sister Ilham, 14, was the only teenage girl in a camp overwhelmingly comprised of young men. She had to go everywhere with her parents and said she was very depressed and lonely. "It's very hard for me. I cannot go outside. I cannot go to the dining room. I cannot go shopping or swimming. I [only] go with my family."

When the interview was over, I took a picture of the family outside their room. The expressions on the faces of the children were hauntingly sad.

From the Afghan families, I went to visit some of the young Iraqi men, including two Marion Le had told me about, Abuozar al-Salem and Monawir al-Jaber. Salem exuded an inner strength but said he could not understand why he was not believed or able to stay with his brother in Australia. In stark contrast, Jaber, skinny and withdrawn, appeared to be hanging on by a thread. He was sixteen when he left Iraq and told me how he had discovered while in offshore detention that his mother had been murdered. The news was conveyed by his brother, who had been accepted as a refugee and was living in Sydney. "The detention camp is a small jail and the island is a big jail. All of the island, same jail. I want to get freedom," he said.

While Houda al-Massaudi was in Melbourne with her husband for treatment, the only other Iraqi woman in the camp was Wahida al-Timimi, who was there with her husband Razak. She greeted me with an impassioned monologue. "I come in 2001. Now 2005," she said. "I very, very tired. No can sleep, no can think, no can eat. Three years and six months in here. Why? Our suffering here is too much." Wahida said she spent her days in their small room and relied on sleeping tablets at night. She had been flown to Australia for one operation and said she needed another. Razak had a blood pressure monitor and was taking several medications. Showing three packets of pills, he said: "I take this for sleeping at night. This for blood pressure. This for heart." Recently he said he discovered his wife unconscious with her eyes open and thought she was dead. He slapped her to revive her and they spent two hours in the camp medical centre. Wahida said she was also suffering psychological problems. "Sometimes my mind doesn't work. I cannot do anything."

It was then that Shamel Mahmoodi, the man in charge of the camp, placed the only limitation on my visit. He said he would prefer that I worked from the area he had set aside for me and not interview the asylum seekers in their rooms. For the next few hours I sat at a desk and the interviews followed a familiar pattern. An asylum seeker would come in and introduce himself. I would listen to his story, ask questions and take his picture. Many of the stories were familiar, because many of these people had been rejected a year earlier on the basis that they were from Pakistan, not Afghanistan. They insisted they now had proof to support their original claims and hoped it would be considered. Many said they became targets for persecution because of their refusal to submit to the tyranny of the warlords and fundamentalists. As Zahir Dulat Shahi put it: "I am human, like you and others. I wanted to do something good. I had a problem with those who make hell in my country for me." Another common denominator was the resort to medication and the sense of hopelessness and desperation.

Aslam Kazimi was 20 when he attempted to reach Australia on the same ill-fated boat as Ali Mullaie. As a teenager, he said he faced the choice of joining one of the fundamentalist organisations in Afghanistan and killing others, or fleeing. He chose the latter. "If I wasn't here, I would be a warlord," he said. His father had been murdered and he was not sure of the fate of other members of his family, including a young wife. Like so many others, he was taking tablets to help him sleep and despaired about his future. "I forgot everything. There is nothing left for me."

He wrote of the desperation of those in the camp in a letter to the regional representative of the United Nations High Commissioner for Refugees, Neill Wright, who was due to visit the camp the following day:

> As you can see here and this miserable situations by the eyes of your heart we have been living here for years and it is really unbearable for every individual of us in which I and my friends faced anxiety, frustration and another physical or mental illness. Every night I deny going to my bed due to the horrendous nightmares and everyday I feel confused and have too much headache in which I'm thinking that my head is going to burst.

Ali Rezaee was the youngest of the single Afghan men in the camp. He was 17 when his life in offshore detention began and confessed that often, when he became consumed by despair, he would go to a corner of the camp and cry at the sky. "I'm thinking, where are my family? Where are they now? What are they feeling now? They might think that I am dead. They think that they have lost me."

A few months before my visit, Rezaee had expressed his feeling of helplessness in an email to Halinka Rubin, a Polish-born Holocaust survivor who lives in Melbourne and had been a tireless supporter of those on Nauru and in mainland detention. "I was a leaf fallen down from a tree, I have no home, no shelter," the email began. It included these lines:

I am a boy who is powerless and lonely burning inside the fence,
I am a boy who is solitary has been grabbing with discrimination in
the circle of human being.
I am a boy whose brain is full of sorrow. I am a boy whose body is
full of wound feeling of pain, doesn't have rest for awhile.
I am a boy, who just sees dark and dark, and a minute is passing
like one hour, a month is passing like a year. And have no sleep
without tablet, no medicine available for reducing the pain, except
rolling tear on my cheek.
I am a boy who in the mid of night, most of the time lonely sitting
in the corner side the fence, looking at blue sky, at stars, weeping
tears, during that time none is moving around.

Next, I spoke to Arif Ruhani, who was also rejected on the basis that he was from Pakistan. He said his cousin and others in Australia had written letters confirming he was from Afghanistan, but had heard nothing from the department on whether his case was being reviewed. Ruhani explained that his darkest hours were often after others had been accepted and how he had been sustained by the support of Australian friends like Susan Metcalfe. While Ali Mullaie kept himself busy helping the Nauruans, Ruhani focused on the others in the camp. "Whenever my friends need me, I show them how to use the computer. Those who cannot write letters for their friends, I write letters for them."

Much later, I read some of his emails to Metcalfe. In one he described how his world was now as small as a match box, "where is no space for an innocent person like me." In another, he expressed his sense of guilt that, while he had food to eat and support from the outside, he had no idea how his family was coping, or if they were alive. "I feel that I am now worthless for my family because now it is me that I should help them in their hard time, but I even don't know where are they," he wrote. There was also his concern for the children who remained in detention on Nauru. "We have a proverb in Persian that if all the doors are closed but still there would be one open. But for us now I cannot see any door open, all the doors are blocks for us."

Assadullah Qazikhil's was a different story to the others who claimed to be Afghans. He was a military officer in the pre-Taliban regime, but insisted he was not a criminal and had never used a gun against his own people or any others. "I am asking the Australian government to investigate my case," he told me. "If I am not telling the truth, if I was liar, they can put me in a charter plane or anything and they can throw me in Afghanistan without any problem. But first I would like them to investigate whether I am right or wrong."

When I asked why he did not take up the Howard government's offer to return to Afghanistan, his response was compelling. "Imagine, a father of six children and the husband of a beautiful wife? Of course, you would go back if it was safe," he said, later returning to show me a picture of his wife and children.

Then there was Arif Hussaini, who seemed one of the most troubled of those in the camp. "The thing he wants to tell you is that there was a misunderstanding in his case," explained Ali Mullaie, who interpreted his words. "He was mistaken for another person with a similar name. The interviewing officer told him names of sister, brothers, father and mother and the name of the place he was living and it was all wrong." Hussaini told the case officer he had the wrong person, but his case was rejected. He did not know whether the mistake has been recognised and said he could prove his identity and Afghan nationality. "He is thinking there is nothing for him in this world," said Mullaie. "There's no help for him. Only he is getting the tablet for sleeping. Every night he is going to the nurse and taking the tablet for sleeping."

Mullaie was interpreter for two of the other inmates. Qurban Ali Changizi, 25, was another who insisted he has been wrongly deemed to be from Pakistan. "The Afghan embassy can prove he is from Afghanistan. All of his family is there: father, mother, sisters, brothers," said Mullaie. "He left Afghanistan because his life endangered. He needs help. He is young and he is tired of waiting here. It is too long in this detention centre. How is it that thousands of refugees from Afghanistan are living in Australia and 29 people from Afghanistan are left here and rejected? It's not fair."

Ali Jan Jafari was another who seemed lost and withdrawn. "I was 21, but now I'm 24," he said through Mullaie. "He wants to tell the people of Australia that day by day he is losing his mind." Jafari's parents were dead and his only brother had also left Afghanistan, but he had no idea where he was. "He has psychological problem and taking tablets and it is not helping him." Recently Jafari had stepped in front of a car during day leave from the camp and was pulled clear by one of his friends. "His mind is not working," said Mullaie.

In all, my eighteen interviews covered 30 of the camp's 52 inmates, including two young Iraqis who were awaiting decisions some seven months after being reassessed. When, finally, there was no one waiting at my door, I went with Mullaie to his small room, made even cosier because he had inherited a desk and book shelf from those who had won freedom in Australia and New Zealand. Yes, he said, he would still like to go to Australia. "I'd like to say thank you face to face to the people who are helping us, to show them that the person writing to you is not different [from the real person]." Unlike many, perhaps most, of the residents, he chose not to take sleeping tablets. When he could not sleep, he wrote poems in Dari and then translated them into English. After his rejection, he wrote:

I shouted and no one heard my cries,
The universe laughs at my cries,
This load has broken my back,
Every joint in the body is cracking.

In his darker moments, Mullaie feared he has been penalised for trying so hard to improve himself in his years on Nauru. In one email to Le, he noted how an interviewing officer looked surprised at his neat handwriting and appearance (he went to the interview in his school teacher's uniform). "In Afghanistan I did not have the opportunity to educate myself because of bad circumstances, so when I came to Nauru Camp, I got the opportunity," he wrote to Marion Le. "I felt happy and lucky that I could use my time and the facilities in the Camp and could make myself a smart person in this almost three years. It is a real pity that with all my efforts to gain knowledge and be rejected."

Certificates he kept in his room confirmed his completion of IOM courses in electronics and teacher training. Letters from Nauru College testified to his "kind assistance," his expertise as a computer teacher and his willingness to "offer his services for the benefit of the children." But it was little comfort.

The light was fading when I left his room. Some of the asylum seekers were playing volley ball. Several returned to the camp ahead of the curfew and wanted to tell their stories. It was too late. As I prepared to leave I was approached by one young Iraqi man with reddened eyes and a desperate expression. He was taking three sleeping tablets each day, he explained, but still could not sleep or find any relief from his sense of hopelessness. All I could offer was my hand and my sympathy.

When I left the camp, I felt the need to talk to someone about what I'd seen and heard. It had been an emotional experience. Instead, it was back to the Oden Aiwo for sate beef, minus the sate sauce, and a can of Victoria Bitter in an empty dining room.

•

The next morning was my last on the island. Before visiting Nauru College to observe Ali Mullaie in the classroom, I called by Nauru's biggest retail and import operation, Capelle & Partner, and briefly talked to its general manager, Sean Oppenheimer. He supported the efforts of the new government to get Nauru's affairs in order and, like many Nauruans, his perspective on the camp was purely economic. More than eighty locals were employed and their wages were among the highest on the island and supported many extended families. He was hoping for a return to the same sort of numbers – around 1200 asylum seekers – that were there at the peak. "It was good for business. It was good for everybody."

At the school, the power was off, presenting a considerable challenge for those learning computer studies. Although Mullaie was designated as a support teacher, the young woman in charge of the class had deferred to his knowledge and communication skills and he was taking the class. With no electricity, he used the battery powered computer sent to him by the Tarren-Sweeneys to explain desktop publishing to the students. His aim was that, by year 7, his students would be able to design a website. So engrossed were his students that, despite the sweltering heat and lack of air in the classroom, no one moved when the bell signalled play time. It was another ten minutes before he realised the time and called the lesson to a halt.

The principal of the college, Floria Detabene, told me at the education workshop there had been times when Mullaie would show his sadness. "He used to become very pale and we'd know he'd be stressing out and psychologically feeling down, but as the years go by, I think because we made him feel at home, he started improving."

His approach was to keep bad thoughts at bay by staying busy, he told me. "When I'm doing positive things, good things, it brings peace to my heart. When I'm not teaching, I'm preparing myself and learning some more and making myself ready for next time." But there were times when Mullaie locked himself in his room and cried. It was only after he walked me to my car during recess that he confided to me that, like many of the others, he was very close to giving up. I gave him a hug to say good-bye and, for just a few seconds, he clung to me, a vulnerable young man with an uncertain future.

Ali Mullaie and Aslam Kazimi being welcomed at Melbourne Airport
by Dorothy Babb

Photo: Sandy Scheltema, courtesy of *The Age*

CHAPTER 6

Afterwards

How many Afghans, who gave up their claims and returned to their region, only to flee again into Pakistan and Iran, were also poorly served by our decision-making process?

– MARION LE, MIGRATION AGENT

The profile of Ali Mullaie and the accounts of my interviews with other camp residents appeared in *The Age* and the *Sydney Morning Herald* on Saturday 16 April 2005. Under the heading "Nauru's Forgotten Faces of Despair," *The Age*'s front page featured photographs showing the faces of fourteen of those I had written about. Julian Burnside, the QC whose visa was withdrawn as he was about to leave for Nauru in April 2004, was among those who were buoyed by the paper's treatment of the story. It was Burnside who launched a High Court challenge to the validity of the visas that were used as the legal basis for offshore processing on Nauru. "Congratulations on a wonderful coverage of Nauru," he wrote in an email that arrived at 9.52 that morning. "Your article may just achieve what the rest of us have been unable to achieve these last four years."

In the letters pages of both papers, readers expressed their dismay and outrage over the government's treatment of those on Nauru and their admiration for Mullaie and the others. Many of those who wrote, like Elaine Smith, were people who had offered comfort and support to the asylum seekers by correspondence over long periods. "They are thirsty for education, freedom, friendship and safety. They have learnt English, worked in the local school, hospital and television station. They have planted gardens and raised chickens," she wrote. "In our letters we have talked about philosophy, sport, science and movies. They have sent me paintings and embroidery. They struggle to keep a positive attitude and create a nurturing environment for the kids, but now, after so many disappointments, they are fragile. Letters express their anguish. We need to give them a safe and permanent home before it is too late. Australia can only benefit from such new citizens."

Some of those who responded appeared to have been touched for the first time by the consequences of John Howard's border protection policy. Bruce Armstrong of Rozelle was one such person: "As I finished reading about the lost souls on Nauru, the tears were rolling down my cheeks. No newspaper article has affected me like this before."

The following day I interviewed the UNHCR's Neill Wright, who had arrived for his first visit to Nauru on the day I departed. He said the emotional condition of those on Nauru was as I had described it. "They are isolated. They are desperate. They don't know what will happen in their future and it is probably the uncertainty that is damaging to their mental health." He was particularly concerned for the well-being of Wahida al-Timimi, who had no other Arabic-speaking woman to communicate with, and the two families with children. "This is not a place to bring up your children and it is not a place that you can plan for your future."

But what seemed surprising was Wright's acceptance that the vast majority of the 52 who were in the camp when he visited were not refugees. His view was that, after more than three and a half years and several interviews, those who were genuine refugees had been assessed as such and resettled. "The residual are for the very large part clearly migrants. You can't say all, because there are still one or two cases where the process may have been flawed, where they still need further investigation into new information that they have made available."

Even so, Wright said he believed Australia, Nauru, the UNHCR and IOM had a "moral responsibility" to work together to find a solution. Asked about the urgency of finding a solution, Wright said: "There are clearly some who in my untrained, non-medical opinion are stressed, very unhappy and very depressed."

Marion Le, who was in the process of making new submissions on behalf of the Nauru asylum seekers, strongly endorsed Wright's call for a humanitarian solution but emphatically believed most cases would be found to be refugees if they were re-examined. Most of the 29 Afghans were in the same situation as those released the previous week, after four years, from the Baxter detention centre in South Australia, she said, and all were deserving of protection. "Most of them have got relatives and friends in Australia – people who came from the same villages who have now got permanent visas." Le also said several of the twenty Iraqi cases were genuine refugees and the rest should be given humanitarian visas and allowed into the community on the mainland until it was safe for them to return. The two Iranians also warranted permanent protection.

When Amanda Vanstone was asked about Wright's call for a humanitarian solution on the Monday, she was unmoved, asserting there had been voluntary returns to both Afghanistan and Iraq. "These people have all been assessed at least twice and 45 of them three times, and found not to be in need of protection. They could end their time on Nauru by agreeing to return voluntarily. Importantly, the UNHCR itself has found eight people within its current caseload on Nauru not to be in need of protection."

The following day, Labor's shadow minister for immigration, Laurie Ferguson, released a statement that was almost totally devoid of empathy. The conviction of many of the asylum seekers that mistakes had been made in their assessments and that new information backed their claims was now in the public domain. Indeed, much of the information had been there for a long time if only someone in authority had been willing to seek it out. While noting that Wright's visit and the Nauruan government's decision to allow the media access to the detention centre highlighted the need for a humane response, Ferguson declared: "At the outset it must be emphasised that the people involved are failed asylum seekers and that the UNHCR itself states that very few are likely to be assessed as refugees. Equally, they refuse to return to their homelands…"

The one positive was a reaffirmation that the government would consider any new information on the cases and, on this basis, Le and her team pushed ahead with the preparation of submissions. On 17 May, Vanstone announced that an agreement had been reached with Afghanistan to allow the forced return of those whose claims for refugee status had been rejected. The offer of voluntary return, with financial incentives, would be put once again to those on Nauru and in mainland detention centres, and they would have 45 days to give an answer. For those on Nauru, it seemed like another setback, but Marion Le put a positive spin on Vanstone's media statement. It reported that nineteen of the 29 on Nauru who claimed to be Afghan had so far had their claims verified by the Afghan government – and more decisions were pending. This was "heartening news," the migration agent said, given that the basis of many of the rejections in 2004 was uncertainty of nationality.

•

The following week was what John Howard might call a "tilting point" in the long-running debate over Australia's treatment of asylum seekers who arrive without invitation. On 25 May, after working for four years within the government to achieve change, Petro Georgiou proposed his own legislation to inject a dose of justice and compassion into the system. One private member's bill would offer relief to those already in the system; another would replace indefinite mandatory detention with "targeted detention subject to judicial review." Perhaps most significantly, temporary protection would revert to permanent protection.

The next day, Vanstone and her departmental secretary, Bill Farmer, appeared before a Senate estimates committee. It was the first opportunity for non-government senators to question senior officials on the two cases that had most embarrassed the government. First there had been Cornelia Rau, a mentally unwell Australian resident who was unlawfully detained at the Baxter detention centre. Then came the case of Vivian Alvarez, the Australian woman who was wrongfully deported. Both, and some 200 other cases, had been referred to an inquiry by a retired senior policeman, Mick Palmer. Farmer's opening statement to the committee offered almost unqualified contrition:

I want to start by making two things clear. First, we profoundly regret what has happened in some cases. We are intensely conscious that our day-to-day business affects people, it affects their lives, and it is distressing and unacceptable that our actions have in respects fallen so short of what we would want and what we understand the Australian people expect. We are deeply sorry about that...

That leads to the second point. The department has made mistakes. If these mistakes are the results of systems or processes or attitudes, these will be changed. If appropriate, there are also processes under the Public Service Act which I would ensure are applied scrupulously and fairly. But we must all learn from our mistakes.

The Palmer report, released in July 2005, confirmed that the mistakes *were* the results of systems, processes and attitudes within the department, and recommended sweeping change. It found considerable evidence of deafness to the concerns voiced repeatedly by a wide range of stakeholders and identified a culture "that ignores criticisms and is unduly defensive, process motivated and unwilling to question itself." There was also "an assumption culture – sometimes bordering on denial – that generally allows matters to go unquestioned when, on any examination, a number of the assumption are flawed." Examples included the assumption that depression was simply a normal part of detention life, which consequently factored out abnormal behaviour in assessments of individuals' medical and mental health.

Although Georgiou's bills had no hope of passing through parliament, they focused public attention on the areas in most urgent need of reform and forced Howard to consider some fundamental changes. Determined to avoid the prospect of members of the government crossing the floor, the prime minister entered negotiations with Georgiou and three other government backbenchers, Judi Moylan, Bruce Baird and Russell Broadbent. If Georgiou were not a politician, he would have made a very good poker player. He ensured that the talking continued even when it appeared to some that there was no prospect of a breakthrough.

The so-called rebels were putting their futures at risk and they incurred the wrath of several colleagues. Victoria's Sophie Panopoulos was the most strident, accusing them of holding the government to ransom. "If you spit the dummy because the vast majority of people in your own party won't agree with you, and you in effect behave as a political terrorist, well, I think you actually lose credibility," she declared.

But Georgiou and his allies were buoyed by an overwhelmingly positive response from their constituents – and their children. Broadbent's adult daughter Emily rang from Geraldton in Western Australia to say she was so proud of his stand she felt like running down the main street, waving her arms and shouting: "Russell Broadbent's my father!" She also flew to Canberra to be there to show support if her father did have to cross the floor. This scenario was averted when Howard and the four reached an agreement on 17 June.

Under the deal between Howard and the MPs led by Georgiou, families with children in detention would be able to live in the community, time limits would be imposed on decisions, the ombudsman would review cases where asylum seekers had been in detention for more than two years, and those in the community on temporary protection visas who were considered eligible to apply for permanent protection could expect a positive outcome by the end of October. Perhaps most important of all, a top-level committee would be set up to implement the changes, chaired by the secretary of the prime minister's department, Dr Peter Shergold.

While the agreement represented a long-overdue change in Australia's approach, those who were still on Nauru would not benefit directly, as Howard made plain during an interview with the ABC's Kerry O'Brien.

KERRY O'BRIEN: Will this policy change apply to Afghani families with children in Nauru who are, after all – who have been in detention longer than others?

JOHN HOWARD: It doesn't affect people in offshore areas.

KERRY O'BRIEN: So the sympathy you are now displaying for children and their parents in detention in Australia doesn't extend to Afghani refugees in detention in Nauru under our direction?

JOHN HOWARD: I mean if you mean by that are we planning to bring them to Australia to put them in residential accommodation? No. But the conditions of detention in Nauru are somewhat different from what they are in Australia.

KERRY O'BRIEN: So that's OK?

JOHN HOWARD: Kerry, nothing is OK in that sarcastic sense, and you know it's not. But we had a difficult problem to deal with, and we have tried to strike a balance between sensitivity and the national interest and the national interest is certainly served by this country continuing to have a firm mandatory detention policy, and whatever people may say about Nauru, we would never have stopped the flood of boats coming to this country if we had not amongst other things had offshore processing. Offshore processing, along with turning the boats back to the north of Australia, mandatory detention and the excision of islands from the migration zone, all of those things taken together stopped the large number of boats coming to this country and effectively provided that protection for our borders. So I continue to very strongly defend the offshore processing of unauthorised arrivals to Australia.

It was a revealing answer because it omitted several of the reasons why the boats stopped coming: unprecedented cooperation with Indonesian authorities to shut down the people smuggling trade; higher penalties for the smugglers; reduced push factors in Afghanistan and Iraq; and the impact of the SIEV X tragedy in highlighting the dangers of paying for passage on over-crowded and unseaworthy vessels.

When O'Brien asked the prime minister if he had pondered how many children had been seriously damaged by their periods in detention, Howard replied: "Well, Kerry, perhaps their parents should have stopped to ask themselves whether they should have tried to come to this country in an unauthorised way in the first place."

KERRY O'BRIEN: Perhaps their parents were fleeing something far more frightening.

JOHN HOWARD: Well, Kerry, we can go, we can go – I'm very happy to sit here and go through that debate and go through that discussion but there is a fundamental principle involved here which has not been altered and that is that people who come here in an unauthorised fashion must expect a period of detention, and they must understand that they are coming ahead of people who seek to come here in an authorised way, and there are many people in refugee camps, children included, who, if others had not taken their places in the positions available for refugees coming to Australia, would have been here earlier. So that kind of argument can be advanced in relation to people whose opportunity has been denied.

KERRY O'BRIEN: Would you agree, Mr Howard, and we've been over this before, but since you've raised it again, would you agree that people who are facing the possibility of death for themselves and their children aren't necessarily going to think in terms of whether they should or shouldn't queue in a refugee centre in Pakistan or somewhere else for an indefinite number of years, where in fact people are dying in those camps?

JOHN HOWARD: But, Kerry, the reality is that not everybody who has sought to come here in an unauthorised way fits the category of somebody who's genuinely in fear of their life.

KERRY O'BRIEN: The bottom line is that most of these people who come here, the vast bulk of them, ultimately are recognised by your government as genuine refugees.

JOHN HOWARD: But, Kerry, no country can afford to have an unrestricted approach to the entry of citizens of another country into our country, and I mean, we have been over this before...

Indeed we had. The simple, unapologetic message was that the damage done to those who came without authority, irrespective of their circumstances, was an acceptable price to pay for winning the battle with the people smugglers.

The agreement between the Georgiou group and the prime minister was announced the day after Douglas Wood, the Australian who had been held hostage in Iraq, was rescued after six weeks of extraordinary effort on his behalf by the Howard government, his family and the Muslim cleric Sheikh Taj al-Din al-Hilali. Like most Australians, the prime minister was moved by the quiet dignity and unshakable resolve of Wood's brothers throughout the ordeal. He later told an interviewer: "It's to me the most symbolic and moving thing to come out of this whole episode, to see a united family, spread around the world, but nonetheless united in its resolve to help a loved one. It's an age old story but it's a reminder of what life is all about in the end – there is nothing more important than the affection in a family."

The legislation implementing the changes negotiated by Georgiou was introduced on 21 June 2005. While Georgiou conceded that it did not meet all of his aspirations, he told parliament, "It will mean a very substantial improvement in the conditions and wellbeing of refugees and asylum seekers. It responds to the deep concerns of a growing number of Australians that the current system is excessively rigid and harsh and has harmed vulnerable children, women and men. It will usher in a new period in asylum seeker policy in this country, with very real improvements in fairness, transparency and compassion in the implementation of policy."

•

I was watching school football on a Saturday in late May when a call came from Marion Le. Nine of the Nauru asylum seekers had been told their claims were now accepted. Ali Mullaie was among them. So, too, were the Hussaini family, Ali Rezaee, Arif Ruhani, Aslam Kazimi and Zahir Dulat Shahi. Once again, the Nauru camp had provided a setting for extremes of happiness and sorrow as some received the news they had been awaiting for almost four years and others dealt with feelings of rejection and even the prospect of forced return. Arif Hussaini, the young man with the sad eyes, collapsed, unable to cope with another rejection.

Along with expressions of concern for those who would be left was unlimited gratitude to those in Australia who had supported them. Shahi expressed his thanks to Ben Habib in an email:

> I do never forget your moral and ethical obligation and the opportunities you have been dedicated to support me and give me the hopes to be calm and hopeful for the pursuit of my objectives. If I'm happy and still breathing against those overloaded stress and pressures on my mind, it is you that enthusiastically support and encouraged me to maintain in willpower and that is the good consequences that I'm coming to see you to thank you. You all have a special place in my heart and I owe you my lifetime and respect you till the world is a world and until the end of my last breathe.

That afternoon, Le, whose office had devoted countless hours to helping the Nauru asylum seekers for no financial reward, sent a letter to Vanstone seeking a commitment that no Afghans would be removed until she had been able to complete all their submissions and have them considered by the department.

A more detailed letter to Vanstone followed, arguing that an in-depth analysis of more than half the Nauru files had revealed three major areas of concern. First, the files of most of the rejected cases included untested "dob-in" material which should never have been included or given weight because it came from a very disaffected source and had been shown to be fanciful. Second, in a third of the files examined, material had been merged from other cases, suggesting case officers had trouble differentiating one case from another. Finally, two of the files had included negative comments made by interpreters, which was "totally unprofessional."

To Le, the review of the files raised doubts about the quality of the assessments of those who had been rejected, particularly those who had felt pressured into returning to Afghanistan. As she put it in her letter to Vanstone:

> How many of the Afghans who gave up their claims and returned to their region, only to flee again into Pakistan and Iran, were also poorly served by our decision-making process? It would take several hundred more hours of research and investigation to ascertain what happened to the rest of the people processed in 2001 and 2002. What is known, of course, is that they had no legal representation or assistance. I am more than prepared to place all the material at my disposal in the hands of the Commonwealth Ombudsman, a judicial inquiry or a Royal Commission.

This was an issue for another day. The immediate priority was to ensure that those left on Nauru were given every opportunity to be heard and that the nine whose long wait had just ended were warmly welcomed. The nine arrived in Australia on 8 June. Dorothy Babb flew from Sydney to Melbourne to embrace Ali Mullaie and Aslam Kazimi. Both, she said later, were like little children. "I could feel them melt into my arms." Also there for the welcome were Halinka Rubin and Anne Horrigan-Dixon. The raw emotion touched several passengers and reduced a couple to tears. East Arnhem land artist, Wukun Wanambi, who had travelled south for the first Melbourne exhibition of his bark paintings, was in the arrival lounge with his young son, who had never before left the Northern Territory. He added to the poignancy of the moment by giving the two refugees a welcome to country on behalf of the nation's first people.

It had been more than three and a half years since their traumatic rescue by HMAS *Wollongong* and the Customs vessel *Arnhem Bay*. If there was a sense of finality and security, it was transitory. As Kazimi expressed it: "I was the age of 13 years old when I started my journey in the shadow of gun battles from Afghanistan and it is still going on. My journey will not be complete until the time of [my being] reunited with my family." Mullaie found it difficult to express his feeling. "I'm very happy to see all my close friends, but I left my friends on Nauru. Too long time they have been there."

Within a fortnight, as the legislation to implement the removal of the policy's harsher edges was introduced, there was some more positive news. The last family on the Nauru camp, the Rehmatis, were told they would be issued with humanitarian visas and allowed to resettle in Australia. Once they left, there would be no children at the Nauru camp. There was also good news for Razak and Wahida al-Timimi. They, too, were given humanitarian visas. Then, in mid-July, the Massaudis tasted freedom when they were granted two-year humanitarian visas. The decisions meant twenty of those I had interviewed on Nauru – people whose cases had been described as without merit – had now been granted visas, and there were grounds for optimism on the part of the others.

When I asked Vanstone at what point the recent arrivals could begin the process of seeking to be reunited with their families, she replied that, like all TPV-holders, they could apply for further protection towards the end of their current TPV. This meant they could be waiting for three years or more.

Even so, Vanstone's decision to approve the visas highlighted a widening gap between the uncompromising rhetoric of earlier times, particularly that of her predecessor Philip Ruddock, and what appeared to be a new pragmatism and, dare I say it, compassion. Many of those who were told that they would never be eligible for permanency and family reunion because they had transited for seven days in a country where they could have sought protection were now achieving positive outcomes. When I asked the minister how the post-*Tampa* policy could be reconciled with this reality, she replied: "I think the answer goes to a recognition that these people may not have had the freedom of movement to seek asylum in countries where they transited on the way to Australia. The department has been applying the seven-day rule flexibly, recognising that while some asylum seekers may have passed through a country where they could have claimed asylum, some may have been prevented from doing so, for example, because they were under the control of a people smuggler."

It was early days, but it seemed that Georgiou was right to suggest a new era was about to begin, one where fairness, transparency and compassion would be finally on a more even footing with that other policy goal of sending a signal to the people smugglers. A new era, and a new chapter in the story of Ali Mullaie and the others, this one offering more uncertainty but at least the prospect of a happier ending.

References

Introduction

Page 16. Fire investigation: see *Dark Victory*, David Marr and Marian Wilkinson, Allen and Unwin, 2003, p 358. Howard's softer edge: see "Howard Yields to Rebel Demands on Detainees," Michelle Grattan, *The Age*, 18 June 2005.

Chapter 1

Page 18. Howard's message that Australia was not a "soft touch": see "Refugees Stranded at Sea," Louise Dodson, Simon Mann and Kerry Taylor, *The Age*, 28 August 2001.

Page 20. "Don't humanise the refugees": see *Report*, Senate Select Committee on A Certain Maritime Incident, October 2002, p 24. Objectives of the public affairs plan for Operation Relex: Ibid, pp 24–25. Award-winning documentary: *Inside Nauru – Pacific Despair*, screened on the SBS *Dateline* program, 29 January 2003.

Page 28. Verdict in trial of Khaleed Daoed: see "Iraqi Guilty of People Smuggling," Johanna Leggatt, *The Age*, 9 June 2005.

Chapter 2

Page 32. Letter from Jeanie Gibb to Marianne Dickie in the office of the Democrat senator Andrew Bartlett, 19 June 2003.

Pages 33–34. Decision to deny permanent settlement and family reunions: "Refugees Need to Abide by Rules," Phillip Ruddock, *Australian Financial Review*, 25 November 1999.

Page 34. Con Sciacca's comments on people smuggling: quoted in "Backing for Hard Line on Refugees," by Janine MacDonald, *The Age*, 23 November 1999.

Page 35. Ed Killesteyn's testimony on family reunion: Senate Legal and Constitutional References Committee, 6 August 2002, p 23. Andrew Bartlett's observations from Nauru: see section on Nauru in refugee section of Andrew Bartlett's website.

Page 36. UNHCR submission to Senate Legal and Constitutional Committee on the Migration Legislation Amendment (Further Border Protection) Bill 2002. Gabaudan's "practical example" comes from testimony to the Senate Legal and Constitutional Committee, 6 August 2002, p 57.

Pages 37–38. The Department of Immigration, Multiculturalism and Indigenous Affairs's answers to questions: drawn from information given to Sediqa Sarwari on Nauru in Q&A format.

Page 43. Vanstone's response to Ruud Lubbers: see "Life After Tampa: Calling NZ Home," Michael Gordon, *The Age*, 27 March 2004.

Chapter 3

Page 46. "The protesters are not refugees": see Media Release, Senator Amanda Vanstone, 17 December 2003. Vanstone responds to UNHCR review of up to 22 cases: see Media Release, Senator Amanda Vanstone, 24 December 2003.

Page 47. Letter from Marion Le to Amanda Vanstone regarding Amin Jan Amin, 10 January 2004.

Page 48. Letter from Tim Costello to Amanda Vanstone regarding Amin Jan Amin, 1 March 2004.

Page 49. Email from Zahir Dulat Shahi, 24 September 2004.

Page 50. Statement by Ali Reza Irfani, 14 February 2003.

Pages 51–52. Ali Reza Irfani's emails from Pakistan and Iran were written to Judith Quinlivan between March 2003 and December 2004.

Pages 53–54. Rajab's case: from *Deported To Danger, A Study of Australia's Treatment of 40 Rejected Asylum Seekers*, A Project of the

Edmund Rice Centre for Justice and Community Education in cooperation with School of Education, Australian Catholic University, pp 4–5. The full report is available at <http://www.erc.org.au/research/1096416029.shtml>.

Page 54. Amanda Vanstone's response to *Deported To Danger:* quoted from a letter to the *Australian*, 14 May 2005.

Pages 54–55. Formal response to questions regarding *Deported To Danger*, put to DIMIA public affairs by Michael Gordon, received 14 June 2005.

Page 55. *Following Them Home*, David Corlett, Black Inc, 2005, pp 205–06.

Page 57. Dr J. Robert Nave's request for a case to be expedited: letter to Phillip Ruddock, 24 September 2003.

Chapter 4

Pages 61–62. Remarks by Petro Georgiou: *Australian Parliamentary Debates (House of Representatives)*, 9 February 2005, p 156.

Page 63. Amanda Vanstone's comments on people smugglers: transcript, media conference, 23 March 2005.

Pages 63–64. Letter from 29 Afghans in State House Camp on Nauru to Marion Lee, 25 November 2004.

Page 64. Email from Aslam Kazimi to Dorothy Babb, 24 November 2004.

Page 65. Letter from Marion Le to Amanda Vanstone, 24 March 2005. Letter from Robert Illingworth, Assistant Secretary, Onshore Protection, to Marion Le, 18 March 2005.

Pages 65–66. Letter from Marion Le to Robert Illingworth, 29 March 2005.

Page 68. John Howard's comment on "people like that": quoted in "I'll See Us Through, Says Resolute PM," John Hamilton, *Herald Sun*, 8 October 2001.

Page 74. Email from Ali Mullaie to Michael Gordon, 30 March 2005.

Page 74–75. Email from David Adeang to Michael Gordon, 5 April 2005.

Chapter 5

Page 84. Description of punishments for detaineees: email from Nauru asylum seeker to Dorothy Babb, 4 April 2005.

Page 85. Shamel Mahmoodi's comments on punishment: email to Michael Gordon, 17 June 2005.

Page 87. Ali Mullaie's comments to Marion Le: email message, 31 May 2004.

Page 92. Aslam Kazimi's letter to UNHCR regional representative, 14 April 2005.

Page 93. Ali Rezaee's poem: from an email to Halinka Rubin, 5 January 2005.

Page 96. Email from Ali Mullaie to Marion Le, 31 May 2004.

Chapter 6

Page 102. Claims verified by Afghan government: Media Release, Amanda Vanstone, 17 May 2005. See also "New Deal for Afghan Refugees," *The Age*, 19 May 2005. Petro Georgiou's proposals: "Libs Defy PM Over Detainees," *The Age*, 25 May 2005.

Page 103: Amanda Vanstone and Bill Farmer testimony: Senate Legal and Constitutional Committee, 25 May 2005, p 6.

Pages 103–04. *Report of the Inquiry into the Circumstances of the Immigration Detention of Cornelia Rau*, Commonwealth of Australia, 2005, pp 160–65. The full text of this report available at <http://www.minister.immi.gov.au/media_releases/media05/palmer-report.pdf>.

Page 104. Panopoulos comments: "Liberal Divide Gets Bitter and Personal," Michelle Grattan, *The Age*, 16 June 2005, p 4.

Pages 105–07. John Howard interviewed by Kerry O'Brien on the *7.30 Report*, ABC TV, 20 June 2005.

Page 107. John Howard interviewed on *AM*, ABC radio, 20 June 2005.

Page 107–08. Petro Georgiou's speech to parliament on the Migration Amendment (Detention Arrangements) Bill 2005, *Australian Parliamentary Debates (House of Representatives)*, 21 June 2005.

Page 108. Email from Mohammed Zahir Dulat Shahi to Ben Habib, 30 May 2005.

Page 108–09. Letter from Marion Le to Amanda Vanstone, 27 May 2005.

Page 109. Letter from Marion Le to Amanda Vanstone, 31 May 2005.

Page 111. Email from the office of Amanda Vanstone to Michael Gordon, 22 June 2005.

Acknowledgements

This book was made possible by the cooperation and support of many people, particularly Marion Le, the migration agent who worked tirelessly with her assistants to achieve justice for those hurt by the Pacific Solution, particularly those on Nauru. Kate Durham accompanied me to the Maribyrnong Immigration Detention Centre to meet a Nauru asylum seeker in 2002. Pamela Curr introduced me to the Alsaai family and to Houda and Khairy al-Massoudi. Susie Strehlow, from the Victorian Foundation for Survivors of Torture, introduced me to Faris Kadhem Shohani. The Fitzroy Learning Network, the Asylum Seekers Resource Centre, Rural Australians for Refugees and Foundation House all provided assistance. Many Australian "mums" and supporters of the Nauru asylum seekers provided valuable insights and information. They include Jeanie Gibb, Halinka Rubin, Dorothy Babb, Elaine Smith, Susan Metcalfe, Georgina Tarren-Sweeney, Emily Williams, Tarni Simms, Ben Habib and Anne Horrigan-Dixon. The names of others who have helped are clear from the text. Most importantly, I acknowledge the willingness of the refugees to tell their stories, often in very difficult circumstances and after enduring great trauma.

Thanks also to the *The Age* for its support; to Harry Gordon and Peter Mares for reading the manuscript; and to Peter Browne, once again, for coming up with the idea for this project and seeing it through.

Also in the **BRIEFINGS** series

Refuge Australia:
Australia's Humanitarian Record
by Klaus Neumann

Winner of the 2004 Human Rights Award for Non-Fiction

Supporters and critics of the Howard government's tough stand on refugees argue that Australia has a proud tradition of sheltering refugees. Yet the record shows that Australian responses to various international refugee crises were motivated by self-interest rather than humanitarian concerns.

Klaus Neumann pieces together the stories of a wide range of people who sought refuge in Australia between the 1930s and the early 1970s, and the government policies that developed in response. He shows the great variety of backgrounds and experiences of the thousands who arrived, legally and by other means, over those four decades. And he reveals the behind-the-scenes debates and decision making that had an enormous impact on refugees and asylum seekers from around the world.

"In the midst of widespread community debate about Australia's current treatment of refugees and asylum seekers, Refuge Australia *provides an important historical context in which to examine these issues. It's also a great read."*

– JUDGES' CITATION, 2004 HUMAN RIGHTS AWARD FOR NON-FICTION, AUSTRALIAN HUMAN RIGHTS AND EQUAL OPPORTUNITY COMMISSION

Also in the **BRIEFINGS** series

The Case for an Australian Bill of Rights: Freedom in the War on Terror
by George Williams

Throughout the world the fear of terrorist attack has fuelled new laws and controls, putting at risk fundamental rights and freedoms. Australia is no exception. But unlike every other western nation we have no Bill of Rights to counter-balance threats to civil liberties. Australian governments retain the power to override the human rights and anti-discrimination legislation we take for granted.

In this important book George Williams outlines the case for a national Bill of Rights to guarantee the rights of all Australians. Surveying the federal government's response to September 11 and the Bali attack, Williams shows how the threat of terrorism makes the protection of basic rights more, not less, urgent. He examines other recent controversies, discusses the Australian Capital Territory's innovative Bill of Rights legislation, and spells out a realistic program for change.

Vividly argued and persuasive, this is a vital contribution to the debate over how Australia should respond to the terrorist threat without compromising basic rights and freedoms.

"Williams seeks, in a succinct and practical way, to set out the background to the rights debate, place it in an historical context, outline pressing areas of present concern and suggest a blueprint for a local Bill of Rights. In all this he succeeds admirably."
– KEN BROWN, *ALTERNATIVE LAW JOURNAL*

"George Williams presents a strong case for an Australian Bill of Rights."
– MATTHEW STUBBS, *POLICY*

Also in the **BRIEFINGS** series

The Politics of Medicare:
Who Gets What, When and How
by Gwendolyn Gray

Despite its promise to preserve Medicare, the Howard government
has created an unworkable two-tiered health system. In this timely
book, Gwendolyn Gray shows how Medicare Plus, the government's
controversial reform package, further undermined the most basic
element of the system, universal access to health care.

Disputes about public versus private health insurance have raged in
Australia for over fifty years. The Howard government has followed
in the path of previous Coalition governments, steadily privatising
the system. Yet international evidence, especially from the
United States, shows that a heavy dependence on private financing
means higher costs and less access, especially for those who need
services the most.

In **The Politics of Medicare**, Gwendolyn Gray explains how
Australia's health system works. She tracks the Howard
government's changes and shows how Labor has supported some of
the Coalition's privatisation measures. And she spells out the
policies necessary to make Medicare sustainable and restore its
fairness and efficiency.

Also in the **BRIEFINGS** series

Indonesia's Struggle:
Jemaah Islamiyah and the Soul of Islam
by Greg Barton

Indonesian authorities responded quickly to the Bali bombing,
tracking down leading Jemaah Islamiyah figures and bringing them
to trial. Despite a subsequent attack in Jakarta, the attention of
many people in the west has shifted to the Middle East and
potential threats to Europe. Yet JI has the potential to mount new
terrorist attacks and destabilise the world's largest Muslim country.

In this timely book Greg Barton traces the religious, cultural and
political development of JI, and argues that it has important
features in common with other organisations linked to al-Qaeda.
Based on extensive research in Indonesia, the book assesses the
level of support for JI and examines the Indonesian government's
success in dealing with the threat it poses. Barton argues that,
while the Indonesian authorities reacted well to the events in Bali,
their subsequent response has not been as effective as is commonly
assumed. He analyses the presidential election results and looks at
the challenges facing Indonesia's new leader.

"*Since 9/11 there has been a distinct genre of books seeking to
provide an insight into the 'new terrorism.' Very few have been able
to balance readability and the complex nature of the phenomenon
and Greg Barton's* Indonesia's Struggle *is one of them. The book is
an insightful and succinct analysis of the ideological origins of JI
and the nature of radical Islam in Indonesia.*"

– TONY LeRAY-MEYER, DEFENDER, THE AUSTRALIAN DEFENCE ASSOCIATION

Also in the **BRIEFINGS** series

All the Way with the USA:
Australia, the US and Free Trade
by Ann Capling

When Australia signed a free trade agreement with the United
States, Prime Minister John Howard hailed it as an historic
achievement that would add "enormous long term benefits to the
Australian economy." Senator Bob Brown called it "a disaster."
No trade agreement has aroused greater controversy in Australia's
history. It affects domestic policy in areas such as culture, public
health and copyright, while producing only meagre gains for
Australian exporters. It represents a departure from the
longstanding bipartisan commitment to free trade between all
countries in favour of special deals between "friends."

Ann Capling traces the evolution of Australian trade policy and
examines the key issues raised by the agreement. Why did Australia
agree to a deal that so patently failed to meet the government's
own objectives? How will the agreement affect relations with our
other trade partners, especially those in East Asia? What are the
implications of linking trade and security? Will the agreement
strengthen our ties with the United States, leading to more
investment and jobs in Australia? Or will it diminish our capacity to
provide social programs that reflect Australian values?

Also in the **BRIEFINGS** series

Disarming Proposals:
Controlling Nuclear, Biological
and Chemical Weapons
by Andy Butfoy

Weapons of mass destruction – or WMDs - have captured headlines around the world. But how useful is the term? According to international relations specialist Andy Butfoy, the constant talk of WMDs is simplistic, misleading and politically manipulative. In this timely book he looks at the reality of nuclear, biological and chemical weapons, providing an overview of who has these weapons and what they are capable of.

Dr Butfoy describes the main pillars of the global non-proliferation regime and the political foundations that underpin it. He explores the challenges facing efforts at controlling WMD, including the potential for "virtual" proliferation, the need to deal with non-signatories and tighten up inspections, the difficulty of enforcing international rules, and the impact of US unilateralism.

"Andy Butfoy's careful dissection of the many and complex arguments that swirl around debates over weapons of mass destruction is a model of clarity. A judicious exposition of the key issues, it makes the case that arms control has played a more important role in preventing WMD proliferation than many realise, but argues that far more needs to be done if the threat of proliferation is to be kept at bay."

– ANDREW MACK, DIRECTOR OF THE HUMAN SECURITY CENTRE, UNIVERSITY OF BRITISH COLUMBIA, AND FORMER DIRECTOR OF STRATEGIC PLANNING IN THE OFFICE OF THE SECRETARY-GENERAL OF THE UNITED NATIONS

Also in the **BRIEFINGS** series

Selling the Australian Government: Politics and Propaganda from Whitlam to Howard
by Greg Barns

Governments spend millions of taxpayers' dollars monitoring every word their opponents utter, gathering ammunition for party political purposes. They distribute political propaganda across the land, at public expense, via the offices of their own parliamentarians. Yet, despite its damaging impact on the democratic process, these practices have rarely been questioned by the media, and are seldom challenged in parliament.

In this forthright critique of the government propaganda machine, Greg Barns – a former senior government adviser – provides a vivid insight into the way governments sell themselves, both publicly and behind the scenes, and how their expensive media management effort affects the political process.

This is a timely examination of a phenomenon that has significant implications for the health of our democracy and our level of trust in government and political leaders.